Social Media Marketing

Turn your Online Presence
on Facebook, Instagram,
Youtube and Twitter
into a Money Printing Machine -
Branding Strategies for Beginner
and Expert Digital Marketers

By John Shackelford

The following Book is reproduced below with the goal of providing information that is as accurate and reliable as possible. Regardless, purchasing this Book can be seen as consent to the fact that both the publisher and the author of this book are in no way experts on the topics discussed within and that any recommendations or suggestions that are made herein are for entertainment purposes only. Professionals should be consulted as needed prior to undertaking any of the action endorsed herein. This declaration is deemed fair and valid by both the American Bar Association and the Committee of Publishers Association and is legally binding throughout the United States. Furthermore, the transmission, duplication, or reproduction of any of the following work including specific information will be considered an illegal act irrespective of if it is done electronically or in print. This extends to creating a secondary or tertiary copy of the work or a recorded copy and is only allowed with the express written consent from the Publisher. All additional rights reserved. The information in the following pages is broadly considered a truthful and accurate account of facts and as such, any inattention, use, or misuse of the information in question by the reader will render any resulting actions solely under their purview. There are no scenarios in which the publisher or the original author of this work can be in any fashion deemed liable for any hardship or damages that may befall them after undertaking information described herein.

Additionally, the information in the following pages is intended only for informational purposes and should thus be thought of as universal. As befitting its nature, it is presented without assurance regarding its prolonged validity or interim quality. Trademarks that are mentioned are done without written consent and can in no way be considered an endorsement from the trademark holder.

Table of Contents

Introduction

Social media marketing has become one of the main tools businesses have to promote their products and services. This should not come as a surprise, considering we are spending the majority of our time on Facebook, Instagram and Youtube.

What is not a given, though, is the fact that most companies and personal brands do not have a proper online presence. In fact, oftentimes their "social media marketing strategy" consists of just posting random content on their website, hoping to get some organic traffic and sales.

The bad news is that this approach does not work anymore. The good news is that not a lot of businesses and solopreneurs have not made the switch to a more programmatic and systematic approach to social media marketing yet. This gives a big advantage to those that are willing to put in the work now and build a strong and solid online presence for their company or personal brand.

In this book, you will discover everything there is to know about an effective and powerful social media marketing strategy. From the basic concepts to the more advanced tactics, each step of the way will be presented with a clear goal in mind: monetization.

The ability to actually convert users into clients is what distinguishes a good social media marketer from a social media enthusiast. The first one is focused on generating revenues for the company or for himself, if he is building a personal brand. The second, instead, believes that likes and comments will help him pay his bills. You have to decide in which category you want to belong to, but we can assure that everything is much easier for your business when you are able to convert leads into paying customers like clockwork.

That is why we decided to write this book. We had enough of all the "Gurus" out there that are selling you expensive books and programs with the promise to teach you their "special weapon". The reality is that there is not a secret to social media marketing. Everything has already been said time and time again.

However, nobody has ever put together a book that goes into the little details of every aspect of this fascinating world. We wanted to do just that, leaving nothing on the table. Every information you need to turn your social media presence into a money making machine is contained in this book.

We are happy to have you on board with us for this amazing journey, we are sure you will learn a lot.

To your success!

Chapter 1

Basic Concepts

Social media marketing is a powerful way for businesses, professionals and organizations of all sizes to find and connect with returning or potential customers or users. Social marketers thus create company Facebook pages and accounts on Twitter, Instagram, Pinterest and other major social networks to reach this goal.

However, not all of these professionals really have clear goals and well defined strategies, nor an in-depth knowledge of how social media interact with consumers and how they can use this interaction to increase brand awareness, boost sales and profits, and create brand loyalty. This is why we strongly recommend that you understand how social media marketing actually works and deeply study the content of this book, as it has everything you need to know to turn your online presence into a money making machine.

Knowing the ABC of social media marketing, having understood exactly what social media marketing is, how it works, how much it requires in terms of time, human resources and budget, is the fundamental premise for those who want to do social marketing in a professional and effective way. This is why it is important to get started by having a clear and exhaustive definition of social media marketing. Knowing the field you are moving on is the best way to avoid big mistakes, especially at the beginning stages. Whether you want to build your personal brand or are looking for resources to boost your company presence online, you cannot skip this first important step.

So, let's get started.

Social media marketing or SMM (also known as social network marketing, social marketing, and, by extension, also facebook marketing, linkedin marketing, etc...) is a branch of online marketing applied to so-

cial networks. This discipline exploits the ability of so-cial media and web-social applications (apps) to ge-nerate interaction (engagement) and social sharing, in order to increase the visibility and notoriety of a brand, a product or service, a freelancer or a public figure. It includes activities such as the promotion and sale of particular goods and services, the genera-tion of new business contacts (which are called "leads") and the increase in traffic to a brand's official website or social pages.

For promotional purposes it is good to integrate a so-cial media marketing strategy with other forms of onli-ne marketing, such as: Search Engine Marketing (SEM), Social Media Optimization (SMO), Social Me-dia Advertising (SMA) or Social ads, and Public digital relations or Digital Pr.

Social media marketing, together with social customer service, social selling and other branches of digital marketing, is considered a component of Social Busi-ness, since it also includes pay-per-click marketing ac-tivities.

Companies and organizations create, or connect to, "networks of individuals" (communities) that share interests and values expressed by the company on social networks. Then, they use these online communities to offer their users relevant content in various formats (mainly text, images and videos) in order to stimulate discussions around the brand.

This is the concrete expression of a very important marketing principle: when people speak about a company, that company can take advantage of the attention, no matter what people say about the company.

In fact, if managed correctly, user and customer interaction with these contents can produce loyalty and social media advocacy. Users and customers, with their "likes", "comments" and "shares" activate word of mouth online by individually involving their network (friends, fans and followers) in the discussion. If you have a company, you know how powerful word of mouth is. Now imagine how big of an impact it can have on your business, when you take it online, where there is virtually no limit on the amount of people one single individual can enter in contact with.
This greatly increases the possibility that a percentage of them ends up becoming a fan or follower of the

company or the brand.

An important distinction: Social marketing or social media marketing?

Sometimes on blogs, podcasts and other online content, social marketing is mistakenly used as a synonym for social media marketing. In reality, social marketing is a popular discipline that became famous in the early 1970s thanks to Philip Kotler and Gerald Zaltman. When we are talking about social marketing, the "product" to be promoted is not a good or a service but is "human behavior". The goal of a social advertising campaign is in fact, for example, to encourage people to protect the environment or to fight against racism.

It is just a simple distinction, but it is important to keep this in mind as in this book we are always referring to social media marketing, not social marketing.

Chapter 2

Advantages and Disadvantages of Social Media Marketing

Now that we have discussed and understood the definition of social media marketing, let's try to understand what benefits it can bring to a company or a personal brand. Here is a list of the main reasons why social media marketing is one of the greatest tools available to anyone that wants to do business online.

- Improvement of customer satisfaction. It has been proven that clients that can get in contact with the brand behind their favourite product are more likely to report a positive shopping experience and become returning customers.

- Increase in customer loyalty (brand loyalty). As mentioned above, people that can see a powerful online presence tend to deem that brand as "solid" and "reliable", which inevitably translates to more money for the company.

- Customer service improvement. Having a good social media presence can help a brand to give a better customer service to its clients by answering their questions directly on the different platforms. Furthermore, this behaviour improves the reliability of the company and helps people that are on the fence to become paying customers.

- Increase in sales leads and sales. As we will see in the coming chapters, social media marketing can be used to actively increase the number of leads and sales, thanks to online advertising tools.

- Increase in web traffic to the company site or

personal blog. This is easy to understand. When you attract the attention of someone, you can redirect that attention wherever you want. Your or your company website is a good choice in most cases.

- Better positioning of your sitei on search engines. This is closely connected with the previous point. When you direct the attention you attract on social media to a website, that website becomes more interesting for Google and other search engines. Therefore, it is not a surprise that social media marketing is also a great way to increase the organic reach of the brand website.

- Increase in brand awareness. This really needs no comment. Brand awareness, as we will see in the coming chapters, is extremely important in this day and age.

- Connection and development of interactive relationships with your target audience. Being able to engage with your target audience is truly an incredible gift, as it allows you to better understand your customers' needs and satisfy them with your amazing product or service.

- Development of a reputation as an expert or leader in the relevant sector (brand authority). By improving your social presence, you improve the view that the general public has of your brand. Think about Apple or Tesla: they have an amazing social presence and they are considered by everyone the leader in their sector.

But is it all sunshines and rainbows?
Well, that could not be farther from the truth. In fact, social media marketing also presents some difficulties to the newcomers, but they are all manageable with the right skills. Before diving deeper, we would like to point out some point of resistance that you or your brand may face when getting started.

- Lack of resources. Social networks are varied and different, consequently the various forms of content (text, video, podcast, webinar, etc.) that have to be published and shared must be adapted to the specificities of each one of them. Likewise, a social media marketing campaign cannot be launched and left alone. It requires time and human resources dedicated to it, in order to be profitable in the long run. This is the reason why, at a certain point, especially for many small companies and personal brands, social media marketing becomes too expensive. By continuing reading this book you will understand how you can reduce the costs, while still building an impactful online presence.

- Negative feedback from your customers. When we discussed the advantages of social media marketing, we stated that word of mouth is an amazing tool to boost sales. Well, that is true if people are talking positively about you. The opposite effect comes when people start giving bad feedback. This can escalate quickly and can lead to a substantial loss of users or clients. You can avoid this in many ways, but the best one is to have a truly amazing product.

Chapter 3

The Importance of Social Media Marketing

S o, we have now come to the most important question of them all. Why should a company or personal brand invest in social media marketing? Let's discuss some points together.

- Low costs. Creating profiles on social networks is free as well as creating and managing social media campaigns with your own social media management team.

- High ROI (return on investment) from advertising costs. The ROI generated by social media advertising is the highest among the various forms of paid advertising. Furthermore, social ads are a type of advertising that allows for high target profiling and personalization. This means that the ads will only be shown to users who are really interested in products or services promoted by the advertiser. This is crucial, as it allows you to cut out everyone that is not in target with what you are offering.

- High conversion rate (CR). More than 51% of social media marketers say that developing meaningful relationships with customers has a positive impact on sales results. This inevitably increases the conversion rate of advertising.

- Improvement of customer insights. Unlike content shared through private channels such as e-mails, instant messaging tools and apps, which are therefore difficult to measure, various social media marketing tools allow precise monitoring of activities on various social networks. From the analysis of the numerous data collected (insight) using tools such as Google Analytics, it is possible to obtain important information on the "sentiment" towards the brand, as well as on the demographic composition, interests, behaviors and needs of customers.

The importance of Social Media Marketing for businesses and personal brands

Why is social media marketing important? Social networks have become a virtual meeting place for people, where:

- they exchange ideas on the most disparate topics.
- they read reviews on products and services they want to buy.
- they look for information on places they want to go, such as restaurants or hotels.

Once, when these social platforms did not exist, this exchange of news took place in clubs or in other social gathering spaces. Today, however, people spend much more time on Instagram, Facebook, YouTube or LinkedIn and that is where they often "meet" and talk to each other. What does this mean? This means that companies and professionals should increasingly work on the ability to intercept and engage users in discussions on online social networks, because in these online environments it is possible to make them become their customers. People's opinions are increasingly influenced by conversations on the internet and this is a fact to take into account if you are selling a product on the web, if you are marketing online, or even if you just want to become important and relevant as an influencer.

Why does this trend affect us? If you are a businessman, or an online marketer, to reach your audience - which is your potential customer base - you must become good at getting noticed where they can find you. And by now you should have understood that that place is online. You must be present and be able to influence the opinions of those who have to make purchasing decisions and you have to do that online, because it is there that purchasing decisions are made more and more frequently.

Chapter 4

Social Media Marketing as a Career

If you are not an entrepreneur that wants to take their company online, but you are just starting to look at social media marketing as a career opportunity, just know that being proficient on social media is also important for those looking for new professional opportunities. This will help you to:

- find a job in a fresh and up to date company;
- be desired by businesses all around the world. In fact, the internet has destroyed physical boundaries and companies look for talents from all around the world, thanks to the possibility given by smart working;

- have career opportunities and increasing earnings. You have to know that social media managers are paid very well, especially if they can provide concrete results to the company they are working for.

To be interesting and attractive to companies, it will also be appropriate to become good at handling the different software, tools and platforms through which you can reach users interested in a product or service on social networks.

Who is the social media marketer?
The Social media marketer (or social media manager) is a digital marketing professional who manages and supervises the social media, digital media and social network channels within a company and acts as a connection between a community of users and the company itself.
He is also responsible for designing the content strategy, managing social media marketing campaigns on Facebook, Twitter and other social networks with the help of the social media team; the creation of an editorial plan with a view to seo; the promotion of products,

services and events, and sharing the contents of the company website or blog. In small and medium-sized businesses, the role of the social media marketer is delegated to figures usually subordinate to him such as:

- Web Content Editor
- Community Manager
- Social Media Specialist
- Digital Marketing Manager
- Digital PR Manager
- Social media strategist
- Facebook Ads Specialist
- Social Customer Care Specialist

Chapter 5

Social Media Marketing in 7 Steps

There are various ways in which a company or organization can do social media marketing. However, all social media marketing activities carried out to be effective cannot be separated from the implementation of an effective social media marketing strategy. But how to define and set up a successful social media marketing strategy?

As in any digital marketing strategy, this is developed through the definition of a social media marketing plan which consists of some precise phases. Let's take a closer look at each one of them.

Please, note that this chapter serves a general structure for the key concept that will be discussed later on in the book.

Step 1 - Conducting a social media marketing audit

In this first step, the audit activity is aimed at evaluating the digital assets (blog, site, app, etc.) available, also in relation to the competition, in order to detect on each social channel what works and what does not work.

In order to simplify this process, here is a list of a few questions that you should aim to answer in this first step. Be as precise as possible, as it will dictate the fundamental aspects of your social media marketing strategy.

- On which social platforms is the brand currently active?
- Which social networks carry the most value?
- What kind of content do competitors post?
- What tone of voice did they choose?
- How much traffic to the website does each so-

cial channel bring?

- What types of content do we post on the different channels? How frequently?
- Are we getting results from investing in social media advertising?

Step 2 - Definition of your social media marketing goals

Having analyzed the digital assets, audience and competition, the next step in establishing an effective social media strategy concerns the definition of goals and results that you hope to achieve (number of leads, customer loyalty, increased sales, brand awareness, etc.)

These goals need to be aligned with the overall communication and marketing strategy so that social media enables the achievement of business goals. In setting goals, to ensure that these will be achieved, it is good to follow the SMART method (specific, measurable, feasible, realistic, as a function of time) used for the first time by Drucker in 1954, in the book "The practice of Management".

Step 3 - Identification of your target audience

You need to be clear who your target audience is so that the message you want to convey on social media is effective. Developing typical customer profiles (buyer personas) is essential for the development of a social media marketing strategy. The collection and analysis of data on the web or from conducting online surveys allow the marketer to paint a well rounded profile of the typical customer. Once the audience has been defined, through surveying activities, they can understand on which social platforms the customer (real or potential) is present.

How do you define your target audience?
We have a dedicated chapter in this book, but let's get a simple idea in order to better understand phase 4.
The surveying activity can be carried out with the help of some social media monitoring tools for marketing automation or manually. Let's briefly see with this last method how to do surveying on Facebook, Twitter and LinkedIn:

1. Write down a list of keywords that are meaningful to you that indicate your product, service, brand or need that you can satisfy.

2. Enter the chosen keyword in the search field of the social network and wait for the results. In the search box you can filter them by "main results", "people", "pages", "places", "groups", "applications" and "events".

3. Enter the following data relating to the comments obtained (date, author, influence, sentiment) in an excel file and store it. This will give you an overview of what is being said online about the chosen brand or topic.

Step 4 - Creating a social media content strategy

Contents are very important in order to create engagement and to achieve your social media marketing goals. With this in mind, it is essential to follow a strategic approach focused on the creation and distribution of relevant and valuable content (Content Marketing), aimed at a clearly defined audience. This is why it is important to do step 3 before starting to produce content without a target audience in mind.

For the communication strategy on the various social media to be effective, however, it will be good to plan the management of these contents. This process is called content strategy and it requires an editorial plan.

For the planning of the editorial plan it can be useful to draw up a matrix of the contents or to use the 80/20 rule of Pareto. In the latter case, 80% of the posts must be used to inform, train or entertain their audience, while the remaining 20% to promote the brand. As for the frequency of publication, given that quality beats quantity, for a small company 2 or 3 weekly contents are generally sufficient. Here are some of the most popular types of content:

- Infographics
- Articles
- Images
- Videos
- Ebooks
- Interviews
- Institutional or corporate news announcements
- Live and virtual events
- Assistance (customer care)

Step 5: Pay attention to Influencers

Research carried out on Twitter shows that 49% of

consumers rely on the advice of Influencers in making purchasing decisions. Finding those who have a large social following for recommendations on the products or services you sell is therefore very important for the success of your social media marketing strategy. One way for a company to gain visibility with social influencers is to use the sharing system suggested by Joe Pulizzi and the Content Marketing Institute, known as Social Media 4-1-1. For every 6 content shared via social media, 4 must be relevant content for your target audience but written by influencers; 1 must be original content created by us; 1 content must be about the sale of your product or service (a coupon for example). You can see how Joe Pulizzi agrees with the Pareto Principle as well.

To engage influencers, I invite you to also take into account any affiliate program to propose to those who are part of your niche. Affiliate marketing, in fact, provides for the payment of a commission to an intermediary, in this case the influencer, for each sale or lead that it manages to generate among its audience. This translates into a win-win situation. The influencer is happy because he can get a portion of the revenues generated and the company is happy because it can get sales without spending money.

Step 6 - Choosing the social media marketing platform

A social media marketing strategy must also be planned taking into account the market in which the company operates (B2B or B2C), the purchasing decision-making phase (social consumer decision journey) in which the customer may possibly be found (research, consideration, decision). Knowing the differences between the platforms and identifying the best ones to support the company's marketing objectives is fundamental. So let's take a brief look at the most famous social networks, not focusing on what these social media are, but in relation to the marketing activities that can be implemented with them.

Facebook

With almost 2.1 billion users and a growth of 15% (year-on-year figure), it is one of the largest social networks in the world. With this social platform it is possible to precisely identify your target audience, create engagement starting from Facebook Groups, easily implement real alternative advertising campaigns to Adwords. The possibility of integrating content in various formats into Facebook is endless and recently it is also possible by clicking on a special button to integrate Instagram content. Users of MailChimp, an email marketing software, can then natively create Facebook ads from their account.

Facebook has many arrows in its bow (Facebook media, Facebook business manager, Facebook live, Facebook connect, Facebook Stories, Facebook news feed ads, Facebook video ads). Let's briefly see the characteristics of some of them:

- Facebook Ads. Advertising on Facebook allows you to reach a conversion rate of 30% higher than other social platforms and allows a decrease in costs per conversion of 50%

- Facebook Places. Is the Facebook geo-location service that allows the user to add information about the place where he is, and based on this, find places, information of interest divided by category (restaurants, shops, entertainment, etc.) and friends who are nearby. The presence of "tiles" or boxes that refer to company fan pages make it a valuable tool for social media marketing activities.

- Facebook media. It is a tool used to teach users who have created fan pages on Facebook to manage them effectively. To access Facebook media just connect to media.fb.com.

- Facebook bluetooth beacons. The social network provides devices applicable to a physical area of your business (beacons) that allow you to send marketing communications (promotional offers, etc.) via smartphone to potential customers who pass in your vicinity. To request beacons, you must register on their waiting list.

- Facebook business manager. Is a free and easy to use tool for advertising and marketing on Facebook. From its dashboard it is possible to monitor the performance of anything connected to your business on Facebook.

Another particularity offered by Facebook is the possibility given to marketers to create effective advertising campaigns aimed at a relatively small audience through Dark Marketing activities. Through a Chrome app (Power Editor) it is possible to create "dark posts" on Facebook. In short, Facebook gives advertisers the ability to create sponsored posts that do not appear on the user's timeline but are accessible to anyone with a direct link or by clicking from an ad.

Instagram

Instagram is a photo sharing application for iPhone, Android and Windows platforms. At the heart of Instagram social media marketing are Instagram stories. They are a way to share photos and videos with your followers that will no longer be visible after 24 hours. Instagram lends itself a lot to social web marketing: people post images and videos, tag friends, insert hashtags and click on content shared by others, making Instagram the social network with the highest engagement rate.

On Instagram it is also possible to post a new type of post called "shoppable post" which includes a special tag that connects the objects in the photo directly to the corresponding e-commerce. Instagram is now testing a new "nametags" feature similar to Snapchat's Snapcodes or Messenger code that makes it easier to acquire Instagram followers. Its "visual" features make this social network suitable for b2b social media marketing, such as travel business, e-commerce and social events.

LinkedIn

LinkedIn is one of the best professional social platforms to connect with your network of collaborators (Linkedin groups) and potential future employers. The social network allows users to import contacts and integrates services such as SlideShare and Pulse. Today LinkedIn is the most popular social network for professionals in the world and is considered the most effective B2B social media marketing and lead generation platform. Like other social platforms, also on Linkedin it is possible to manage advertisements (Linkedin ads). The platform also offers businesses and publishers the ability to natively run video ad campaigns and include videos within their company pages. Through the implemented Linkedin Tracking pixel, it is then possible to measure the number of leads, sign-ups, visits to websites and other actions generated by video ads.

Snapchat

Snapchat is a mobile application that allows users to send photos and videos to friends. Snapchat Stories (collages of photos and videos shared for no more than 24 hours) are a great engagement tool. With the release of the new version of the app, it will soon be possible to share Snapchat stories also on Facebook and Twitter. Snapchat is testing new in-app e-commerce options through its Snap store located within the Discover platform, which could lead to partnerships with companies of all kinds in the future. If your products are aimed at a very young audience, marketing on Snapchat is definitely the right choice.

Pinterest

Pinterest is a popular photo sharing service that allows anyone to create collections and more. 93% of its users use it to plan purchases or to research product information. Marketing activities are possible thanks to Pinterest ads and buyable pins. Pinterest is continuing to grow among small and medium enterprises. The adhesions to its Pinterest Propel program in fact recorded a + 50% this year. With 81% of its 150 million monthly active users being women, topics such as interior design, decoration, cooking and clothing work very well.

Reddit

Reddit is the social network where the community decides what will be more relevant and what to give more visibility to. Reddit has a subreddit (think of it as a digital board) for almost every category. The growth of this social network in the world is due to 2 factors: the AMAs format (ask me everything) and the peculiarities of the voting system. Marketing activities are possible thanks to Reddit ads, however, it is necessary to pay close attention to the large number of comments received and therefore it requires constant attention.

Telegram

Telegram is a messaging application that allows you to chat with contacts, organizing public and private groups, with a series of functions dedicated to visual content. You can add images, emojis, documents, files and links to messages. Companies can use Telegram to notify their clients of new offers and promotions or to directly chat with them if we are talking about a small and close community.

Tumblr

Tumblr is a microblogging platform with social networking features. Much used by fashion brands, bloggers and designers for the publication of very accurate content. People spend more time on this platform than on Facebook, which makes Tumblr a good place to post and advertise.

Twitter

Twitter is another fantastic social media platform that allows users to quickly send 280-character posts through Tweets. These are characterized by the presence in the text of an hashtag (a keyword preceded by the hash symbol #). Twitter marketing is often used by companies to maintain contact with their customers, to promote their brands, products or services, and to obtain information from consumers.

Whatsapp

Whatsapp is one of the most used instant messaging

applications in the world given the ease of use and quality of service. In 2017 WhatsApp crossed the milestone of 1 billion users per day, thus equaling Facebook. The app offers the possibility of interacting with your contacts within conversations and today you can publish, as status updates, temporary Snapchat-style photos and videos. With the release this year of WhatsApp Business, and the coming integration of the possibility of making payment, the brand officially accesses one-to-one marketing.

Disqus

Disqus was born as a commentary hosting service for websites and blogs. This platform now represents a real social network where users can give life to debates or participate in existing ones. To manage comments, just access the platform with the same account used for social media, using the "share" button you can then bring the discussion to your favorite social network.

YouTube

Youtube is a network where users post video blogs, video ads and videos of various genres. For marketers, videos are the ideal medium to share medium to long-form content and Youtube is the go to hosting place for video content.

Step 7 - Measurement and testing

It is necessary to constantly analyze the social media marketing strategies implemented to understand which has been effective and which has not. As part of a social media marketing strategy, it is necessary to decide which metrics or KPIs to use to verify whether the set goals have been achieved. Some metrics to consider to measure the success of a social media marketing strategy are the following:

- Cost per click (CPA)
- Conversion Rate
- Number of followers
- Brand mention
- Total shares
- Impressions
- Comments and engagement

Chapter 6

Social Media Marketing Trends for 2021

Social media are dynamic by their nature and, for this reason, they are characterized by trends and communication methods that can vary over time (ever heard about social media trends). Knowing these trends can be crucial in choosing the most direct and effective social media marketing strategies. Below is a brief description of the social media marketing strategies that, as it seems, will most characterize 2021.

1. Use Tik Tok for your Social Media Marketing strategy. This social network is growing rapidly and is a must for those who want to reach users under 30, which currently represents 66% of the channel's users.

2. Social media wellness becomes essential to create engagement among users. People are gaining greater awareness of the use of social networks and the impact they have on mental health. This is why even the platforms themselves are committed to making the user experience pleasant and not very harmful. If you notice changes in the level of engagement, you should not be scared, but observe your competitors and if they suffer the same reduction you can feel comfortable. People are increasingly trying to reduce their time on social media and leverage the time they spend constructively.

3. Fake news will be limited. This is certainly excellent news and a very positive trend. The fact that fake news is on the decline does not mean that it still does not remain a problem. For those involved in social media marketing this means that the user will weigh heavily what you declare about your company and your products. So, please, maximum transparency!

4. Tightened security. Another growing trend strongly correlated to social media marketing is user security. The recent scandal involving Facebook and Cambridge Analytica is likely to further enhance this trend. The privacy protection measures for users of Social networks will have to be increasingly suitable to fight hacking, identity theft, phishing and various other security threats.

5. A more effective strategy with augmented reality and virtual reality. Technology is taking great steps towards AR and VR and you must be able to adapt to this change. Augmented reality and virtual reality will improve not only the effectiveness of your strategy, but also the experience of your users.

6. The use of artificial intelligence will increase. The use of artificial intelligence (chatbots and virtual assistants) will increasingly allow marketers to interact with consumers in real time and in a personalized way. Facebook is preparing to relaunch a virtual assistant that will be able to offer suggestions to users and answer all their requests through the Facebook Messenger chat. According to Gartner, a world-leading multinational company in strategy consulting, research and analysis in the field of Information Technology

(IT), 20% of business content could be generated this year by machines similar to artificial intelligence. Think about it, of every ten articles you read online, two of them are probably written by a robot.

7. Designing the social media marketing strategy to involve Generation Z. The generation of the future is becoming more and more involved with technology and this requires innovation and creativity from marketers. 2021 will be the year of the challenge to find new ways to entertain and involve the youngest, studying them carefully and understanding their needs.

8. Influencer Marketing. Social media influencers are able to generate a return on investment 11 times greater than any other digital marketing strategy. It is no coincidence that 94% of social media marketers claim to have achieved excellent results thanks to their collaboration and consider them an integral part of their social media marketing strategy.
In recent years, this tactic has been used in many sectors (social media marketing for tourism is an example above all), with results such as to become the main di-

gital channel for many companies. The success and evolution of this tactic has also favored the creation of numerous new professional figures. Among the most sought after we find the social media marketer.

Chapter 7

SMART Method for Goal Setting

Here is a quick overview of the SMART method.

Specific, measurable, attainable, realistic and time effective: this is how goals should be formulated, so that they are effective for the purposes of our planning and organization work. Use the SMART method for formulating goals. In this way, all the criteria that a well-formulated goal must possess will be respected.

The aim is to create an exceptional planning and organization process. Knowing what we want to achieve with our social media marketing strategy is important, but how do we state that clearly so that we can increase the odds of actually achieving our goals?

This is where the SMART method comes into place. As mentioned before, SMART is an acronym and indicates the criteria for the formulation of a goal, which must therefore be specific, measurable, attainable, realistic and have a specific time period.

Specific goals

We often make the first mistake by not reflecting deeply on what we want to achieve with our social media marketing strategy and we favor an inadequately specific formulation of our goals.

Examples of non-specific objectives:
"We want to make more money."
"We want more followers."

What do these statements mean? When is it "in the future"? And how much would you like to increase the number of followers? What does it mean to make more money? Does it refer to sales or profit? Neither objective specifies what the final perspective is. Take this into account when formulating your goal.

The same goals formulated specifically:
"In the next month, we want to increase our monthly revenue by 5% using social media marketing"
"In the next month, we will get at least 1000 more followers on our Instagram page."

Measurable goals
In order to verify the achievement of the goal or to get motivated to work towards it, the goal must be measurable.

Examples of non-measurable goals:
"We want to post beautiful images on our social media pages."
"We want to have good comments on our posts."

What does beautiful images mean? When do you deem a comment as good? Do not leave room for interpretation. Formulate the goal in such a way that it can be verified whether it has been achieved or not.
Examples of measurable goals:
"We want to post images on social media pages that

get at least 1000 likes."

"We want to receive one positive feedback every two customers."

Attainable goals

In order not to give up on your goals, it is necessary that you recognize them as such and accept it. In other words: the goal must be attractive to your or your company eyes.

Examples of unattainable goals:
"During the week we will post 100 times per day."
"In the future, all customer inquiries will be dealt with immediately."

Be honest with yourself. Can you accept these goals? Will they be attractive enough to your eyes even over a period of months? Set goals in such a way that for you personally and for all employees they are actually achievable and remain attractive over time.

Examples of attainable goals:
"We dedicate myself to our social channels consistently, posting at least 5 times per day to create brand

awareness."

"All customer inquiries will be processed within 48 hours."

Realistic goals

In the throes of ambition, we have the feeling of being able to achieve anything. But even then, be honest with yourself. Are you able and are you willing to achieve these goals and keep chipping at them?

Examples of unrealistic goals:
"At the end of the day we always respond to all the comments we received that day."
"From now on we will always refund our customers."

Don't be fooled by your ambition when formulating goals. Stay realistic to avoid bankruptcy in the short term.

Examples of realistic goals:
"We organize our comment according to priorities (1 = urgent / 2 = to be fulfilled within 2 days / 3 = to be fulfilled by the end of the week) and we make sure that at the end of the day we have carried out the tasks of

priority 1."

"We will refund customers that actually are suitable for the refund, based on the contract they signed when they made the purchase."

Time effective goals

Don't leave the deadline of your goal to chance.

Examples of non time effective goals:
"We will post on our social channels."
"We will answer those comments."

You now have unlimited time to do those two things. Sooner or later these goals will be reached. However, you prefer to define in the goal itself the deadline by which you want to reach it or put it into practice:

Examples of time effective goals:
"We will post on our social channels by 9am every day."
"We will answer those comments before lunch."

Think about the SMART method the next time you formulate goals for your social media marketing strategy and write them down. In this way it will be easier for you not to lose sight of them and to achieve them faster.

Chapter 8

Pareto Principle and the Yerkes and Dodson Curve

The Pareto principle is also called the "80/20 law" or the "Pareto effect". Regardless of how you decide to call it, the principle is named after its discoverer Vilfredo Pareto (1848-1923). At the beginning of the 20th century, Pareto, an engineer, sociologist and economist, conducted research concerning the subdivision of popular heritage in Italy. Pareto's research showed that one fifth, or 20% of Italian citizens, had about 80% of the national wealth.

Pareto therefore deduced that the banks should have concentrated on that 20% of Italians to be more efficient and obtain greater profits, thus indirectly establishing that the banks only devote a fifth of their time to assisting the remaining 80% of the population.

The Pareto principle represented the inequality of the division and the lack of balance between the resources used and profit. However, this proportion was also true in other sectors.

- Commerce: 20% of products or customers invoice 80% of earnings.
- Storage: 20% of products take up 80% of the places on the shelves.
- Internet: 80% of data traffic is generated on 20% of websites.
- Road transport: 80% of all journeys take place on 20% of roads.
- Phone calls: 80% of calls are made to and from 20% of the saved contacts

The 80/20 law is best known for its application in time management. Because with a correct setting of your time it is possible to do 80% of the work in 20% of the time taken.

The goal of the rule discovered by Pareto is to achieve the greatest result with the least effort, since a lot of time is often invested in tasks with lower priority. With the right priorities and better time management, however, you can set up your work more efficiently and in a targeted manner. The Pareto principle is particularly suitable for those professional sectors with tight deadlines, allowing you to focus your efforts in the most efficient way possible and to complete the tasks within the established time frame. This 80/20 law is usually associated with other methods of time management, such as the Eisenhower principle.

There are some types of errors that are often encountered in the application of the principle in question. The first is that it is wrongly claimed that with 20% of the time invested, 80% more than normal is reached, thus bringing the yield to 100%. This is clearly a misinterpretation, where the figures are added together, thus leading to 100%, despite the fact that they are actually two different and separate aspects. Commitment and performance are not the same thing and therefore cannot be added together so easily. To generate 100% of the yield you need to commit 100% and that is especially true when it comes to social media marketing.

An interpretation of this type serves no other purpose

than to give false hopes, which are far too optimistic. However, understanding the functioning of the basic principle is not enough to avoid misinterpreting its use. In fact, one might be led to think, always wrongly, that it is enough to reduce all tasks to only 20%. But here too, we must not get confused: many of the jobs that need to be done in social media marketing do not lead directly to the goal, however they are necessary to get there. Writing and replying to emails fall within the duties of this type, which in fact, although they may seem a negligible element and of little relevance to the success of a company, are nevertheless essential.

The Pareto principle serves precisely to optimize those tasks that remain necessary despite generating less or no profit, so as to take away as little time as possible. Any incorrect use of the Pareto principle can lead to the attribution of too low importance to a large part of the work to be carried out. The fact is that only those who dedicate themselves to their work in a conscious, concentrated and structured manner can obtain 80% of the results with 20% of the work done. Social media marketing falls perfectly under this principle.

The 80/20 law is very versatile. It can be used in one's

private life, in study and at work for better time management. In our case, we use it to develop a much more effective and time saving social media marketing strategy. The important thing is to know which activity contributes most to achieving what you want, so as to be able to give the right priority to the various tasks. The Pareto principle helps to make the best choice in this regard.

From a purely theoretical point of view, the Pareto principle can be applied in any sector, not only in social media marketing. It has seen successful application in school and academic training, as well as in everyday life for normal people. Often the 80/20 law is associated with the working life, where it is more usual to have strict deadlines and well defined goals. But even in everyday private life there are many tasks that must be carried out in a short time and as efficiently as possible.

An example for everyday life
In order to understand the importance of Pareto Principle for social media marketing optimization, it can be useful to take a look at a common everyday life sce-

nario.

If friends or family tell you that they will be visiting you shortly, there is little time left to clean up the house. Normally, to put everything in order and carry out all the household chores, it usually takes three hours, but in the case of such a visit, it often takes no more than an hour and a half. For this reason, following what is determined by the Pareto principle, it is initially advisable to focus on those that contribute to the well-being of the guests. Collecting objects and clothes around the apartment, putting dirty dishes in the dishwasher and cleaning the table is part of these chores.

The rooms most often used by guests are the living room, bathroom and dining room, and are therefore the ones on which you need to focus initially. Cleaning these rooms practically corresponds to the aforementioned 80% of "success", while one's bedroom, cellar and the like alter the mood of guests to a lesser extent. In social media marketing this translates, for instance, into taking care of the most important customer requests first, prioritizing them over the less urgent ones.

Yerkes and Dodson curve

Similarly to the Pareto principle, Yerkes and Dodson law also has to do with the relationship between commitment and productivity. The curve in question takes its name from psychologists Robert Yerkes and John Dodson. From their research it emerged that productivity improves proportionally according to the growth of the commitment, at least until the maximum point is reached, or the point where the improvement in performance reaches its maximum, thus leading to a decrease in productivity.

The Yerkes and Dodson curve is represented by an inverted U. Despite continuing to invest time and energy, productivity inevitably begins to decline once the top is reached. The high pressure and the resulting stress cause a decrease in performance, leading to worse results. Like the Pareto Principle, the Yerkes and Dodson law also affirms, or rather confirms, that only a certain part of the commitment leads to most of the productivity. The remaining effort required to achieve 100% results leads to very little in terms of productivity.

Chapter 9

Identify the Correct Buyer Persona

As for every concept we introduce in this book, let's start by giving a detailed definition of what a buyer persona is and what it is not.

Buyer personas are fictitious representations of typical customers of a company, created on the basis of data collected through surveys or interviews, taking into account not only their socio-demographic, psychographic and behavioral characteristics but also data, quotes and sayings that can be useful for creating ad hoc products and services.

These are archetypes or models that result from insights provided by consumers and users. Making use of buyer personas therefore means starting from the study of real customers to guide business and marketing strategies that will lead to the involvement, conversion and loyalty of new buyers. The insights collected may concern various types of data, such as personal information, expressions used, ways of speaking and quotes, taken during interviews, which allow us to illustrate in a more "human" way, thus going beyond the numbers and statistics relating to purchases and preferences, the "type" of person who visits a site, page or shop.

All the information collected and analyzed makes it possible to create archetypes from which brands can align their marketing strategy and brand positioning based, therefore, on the expectations of current customers and potential buyers.

The identification of buyer personas includes the collection and analysis of socio-demographic data, data relating to purchasing habits, payment methods, and much more. These are in fact useful information but not exhaustive if you intend to accurately identify the customer or the typical user of a business. As many expert explain, very often when we try to identify the target we mainly think about a demographic target. Maybe we think about the gender, the age group, the geographical area which our users come from. The reality of the facts is that what works in terms of communication is not so much knowing this information but what the behavioral and motivational data of the macro-groups and segments of users who arrive on our site are.

Knowing what their problems are and how they would like to solve them is useful, as it allows us to collect data relating to the value system of users or customers in order to create targeted content that meets their way of thinking and to conceive of reality.

The use of the term personas, intended as the creation of typical profiles of users who visit a website, is attributed to Alan Cooper, software designer and programmer who, thanks to his experience in the field, has developed and studied over the years the application of this methodology to the design sector for the creation of user-friendly software. The result of these researches was initially published in 1998 in "The Inmates

Are Running the Asylum", a book that introduced the concept which then spread widely in various sectors.

The reason behind the construction of a buyer persona

These profiles are useful for guiding the decision-making process relating to multiple aspects of the business, such as the creation and definition of the characteristics of products, services and store, the definition of the structure and layout of a site, as well as marketing strategies. Furthermore, they help identify the correct brand positioning to be adopted to communicate our services and products in an appropriate manner to the various customer groups.

The traditional approach of identifying the target of a product, service or message is based on the collection of mainly quantitative data, obtained thanks to statistical analysis and socio-demographic information, but also related to purchasing behavior and preferences by channel communication.
However, this type of survey is not enough to identify the psychological nuances of the average customer or user of a site, as many marketing experts have explai-

ned during the years. In fact, as the expert explains, even if the definition of the target is essential to understand what to focus the company resources on and to identify the aspects of the business that need to be optimized, this only allows to clarify " what" to propose, but not "how" to offer it to customers. In fact, in planning a marketing strategy it is necessary to create content aimed at the different targets of the business, since a generalist and not very personalized communication cannot be in line with the way of communicating and reasoning of different customers and, therefore, it will be difficult to respond. to different doubts, worries and needs.

To better understand your target and create content that is truly relevant to potential customers, it is advisable to think like them and try to identify with the different buyer personas and their "thought structures" as David Meerman Scott explains in the aforementioned book. In the same book, the author explained that "the idea behind the concept of buyer personas is to understand your target so well that you practically start to think like him".

Design the perfect buyer persona for your company

The creation of these archetypes allows us to understand who the customers or users of a site are, but also the way they think, what they want to achieve and what are the objectives and reasons that guide their behavior, in addition to the methods and timing of purchase. To construct the identikit of the ideal customer or user, it is necessary to take into account different types of information relating to consumers and proceed with the collection of data through survey tools that allow you to listen to customers and then, in a subsequent phase, process the data that will allow to identify and construct the different buyer personas in an accurate and detailed way.

What data to collect

In the collection of data for the construction of the representations of the customer or the ideal user of a site, we range from the most personal information (such as socio-demographic, psychographic data, etc.) to those that instead relate more specifically to any response, approach or preference of the typical customer towards a product, a site or a company.

Socio-demographic data

Socio-demographic data allow you to "empathize" with buyer personas, giving them a human form, a face and an identity. Therefore, we are talking about information such as age, sex, origin, level of education, employment and income, as well as data relating to marital status, the number of children and the family unit. It is no coincidence, then, that Meerman Scott recommends giving a name to the buyer personas, precisely because these types of data allow you to "humanize" your company and related marketing strategies. Establishing that, for example, we must turn to Jane, a 37-year-old woman from New York, with more than one child and happily married, is useful to make the image that professionals have of a specific target group less abstract. This will simplify and identify the correct way they must address the communication of the brand or product.

In some cases, it may also be crucial to know the skills of the customer or typical user of our site. For example, the development of the design of a site or software or the versions of a site in different languages may vary depending on the target who in fact may be particularly familiar with those tools or may instead be a beginner. The same thing is true for linguistic skills. You have to ask yourself if a specific target group on the site knows the English language or if it is necessary to create a version in other languages as well. This, in particular, is something to be taken into consideration very seriously, especially in this multiethnic world.

Psychographic data

To understand how a certain type of customer thinks, it is also necessary to carry out a psychographic analysis, taking up elements that make it possible to identify some personality traits, attitudes, ways of thinking and typical saying of a particular buyer persona. For example, it would be appropriate to understand if it is more or less extroverted, if it is impulsive (which can affect the type of purchases and the impact of advertising communications), if it is particularly emotional or more rational, if it is more or less tending to savings, etc.

In addition to the preponderant character traits, we must also ask ourselves what fears, anxieties or frustrations can be. Think of a company that produces toys and the importance of identifying the greatest concerns of parents for their children. This, however, is not enough because it is useful to understand what leads them to buy that product. For example, parents could aim to buy a more "educational" toy, asking for opinions in the store or doing online searches, while grandparents could aim to please the child, deciding to buy a toy advertised in a TV commercial, perhaps even more expensive but which can satisfy the grandson's requests. This information can be useful in making decisions regarding the characteristics of the product, the price, but also the tone of voice of the advertising messages, therefore depending on the buyer persona to whom it is addressed.

Another important aspect concerns the predominant system of values for each buyer persona, that is, what are the moral principles not to be infringed, what kind of communication or marketing action could against the ethical principles of a specific type of consumer. In this regard, as many experts explained over the years, it is necessary to identify the values that our brand or our site must keep alive in order not to go against the moral values of the users to whom it is approaching. Why? because, if on the one hand we are quite inclined and available to a change of opinion on certain ideas or concepts when someone (such as a brand) tries to convince us of something, on the other hand there are certain principles or values to which we are not willing to give up. One thing is certain values do not change and, on the contrary, we feel a sense of disgust and anger towards those who try to transmit moral values that are different from ours. Discover the value of your ideal customers and build your social media marketing strategy on them.

Furthermore, it is necessary to take into account not only the values but also any prejudices or preconceptions, conventions and opinions that people have regarding the most varied topics that can in some way interfere with the evaluation of a product or an advertisement and must be identified. and taken into consideration.

Needs, motivations and objectives of the buyer personas
Knowing the motivations, priorities and needs that lead customers to seek a specific solution, to solve a

problem, to find out about the different brands that offer a certain service or to buy a certain product is essential to know what to focus economic efforts on identify the elements or characteristics to be highlighted in the communication of a product or brand.

On Alan Cooper's website, Kim Goodwin mentions the different types of objectives or expectations of the buyer persona that should be identified and which must affect the design of sites, products and planning of marketing strategies. The expert refers above all to life goals, such as retiring at 45. This particular goal may not be of great relevance to anyone designing a phone, but it may be useful for someone who is creating a financial planning tool.

Limits, problems and barriers to purchase
Another important element to analyze in detail is the perception that customers have of the brand or its products. Knowing the preconceptions, opinions and criticisms that consumers have to move to a given solution will allow brands to respond accordingly, proposing changes based on the various problems identified. Furthermore, once any obstacles to purchase have

been identified, that is, anything that could lead a customer to decide that they no longer want to buy the product or even try it, companies can create a communication that allows them to overcome these obstacles.

Decision criteria

What criteria do different customers or users focus on for purchasing decisions? Knowing what drives consumers to choose one brand to the detriment of another is of great importance for companies, since it allows you to understand not only what the advantages that make your product essential for a specific target are, but also the problems that make it so that it prefers the solution offered by a competitor.

Buyer journey

The analysis of the buyer journey is essential first of all to understand which are the points of contact with the company that will allow you to reach the customer effectively, inspiring trust and meeting the preferences for the use of content and research of the information. It is necessary to know the process or the path taken by customers before arriving at the purchase of the product, so as to understand what difficulties or problems there are and how to overcome them effectively.

It is therefore of great interest to obtain data on all the obstacles that can intervene in the purchase process. How can you do this? For example, you can achieve this by asking the user the type of sources they use when looking for information on products or services and through which channels they usually receive or would prefer to receive commercial communications. Remember, if you control the journey of your customer you control your customer.

Effective tools for data collection
There are several tools that allow you to collect the information needed to build buyer personas. Social media, and therefore tools such as Facebook Audience Insights but also Google Analytics, can be very useful for collecting large amounts of demographic data, as well as the times in which each group of users is most active on the web, their geographical origin and related interests.

In addition to the processing of statistical data relating to personal data or purchasing behavior, the carrying out of interviews is particularly important because it also allows you to analyze the type of language used by the buyer personas and therefore understand the style of communication, the words, the terms that may hit them more. Therefore, it may be useful to extract from these one or more representative quotes of each buyer persona, their motivations, fears, aspirations, expectations towards brands or products but also their life goals, for example. On the basis of this information, short bibliographic descriptions can be constructed that can serve as inspiration for the creation of content aimed at that specific group of customers. You can also use online surveys sent via email through, for example, Google Form.

How to analyze the data you collect

Once the data has been collected, how to put them together to create the identities of the ideal customer or the different types of customers? As for the ideal number of buyer personas, according to David Meerman Scott, it must be identified "on the basis of the factors that differentiate them".

For example, some companies may have a different profile to represent the Asian, European and North American customer, thus creating different archetypes according to the different geographical areas in which it operates. It all depends on the sector, the type of company and business you offer, as well as the different target groups involved.

Chapter 10

Content Strategy: Everything You Need to Know

Content strategy and content marketing are often confused and used as synonyms, but they are and remain well-defined elements with the first being hierarchically superior to the second. In fact, we will see how a content strategy can exist without even a glimpse of content marketing. Because "content is king" remains a valid dogma, but there is no king without a kingdom that has precise borders within which to exercise its hegemony.

Before diving deeper into content marketing, it is important to give a definition of what we are talking about and distinguish content marketing from content strategy.

Content marketing - definition
Content marketing is the creation and dissemination of useful and valuable content, aimed at a well-defined audience, with the aim of attracting it, acquiring it and inducing potential customers to take profitable actions.

Content strategy - definition
Content strategy deals with the planning aspects of content management throughout its life cycle. It includes the analysis phase, the alignment of the content with the business goals, influencing its development, production, presentation, evaluation, measurement and archiving. What the content strategy is not, however, is the content implementation phase. Practical development, management and dissemination of content are the tactical results of the strategy, what needs to be done for the strategy to be effective.

Thus, Rahel Anne Bailie, a famous content strategis, in

an article on her blog dated 2009 but still valuable, stated this exact difference.

Basically, the two phases are split. The first one involves strategic planning and the second one, which is subsequent and regulated by the first, involves the creation and share of the content in its different forms.

Content strategy is what lies upstream, it is the planning activity that defines and regulates this process. The difference lies in the fact that the content strategist does not deal with the production of content but turns his attention to the planning of the same, not limiting himself to defining when they should be published but above all why they should be produced. Each content, in fact, must be a single brick useful to build the bigger building. It is a work of engineering and architecture for which not only workers and concrete are needed, but first of all a clear, defined project divided into several phases. Without precise planning, clear goals to strive for and measurable objectives to be achieved, the contents will be ineffective and self-referential. They simply won't "stand up", exactly like a building built in the absence of a blueprint.

Content strategy and content curation

As evidence of how much and how the content strategy has an absolute value greater than content marketing, there are numerous examples of strategies of extraordinary success without even the production of their own content. In this case, we leverage on content curation (defined as the ability to filter and add value to the contents we receive daily from all online sources, i.e. the process of selection, collection, organization and subsequent sharing of content relating to a particular topic or subject area).

We can offer useful content to potential customers that are simultaneously in line with our business goals. We are referring to reporting, commenting and rewriting articles written by third parties that thus enter the information sphere of our audience. In this way, we will add a valuable contribution capable of underlining our expertise in the field, the relevance of the subject for our industry and the usefulness of that information for those who receive it.

Structuring a winning content strategy

In a broader marketing action, whether it is inbound

marketing or social media marketing, content remains the main focus or at least it should. In defining the strategy, a good content strategist can and must make use of numerous tools and suggestions to identify topics of interest. Among these, in addition to what a paid platform like Hubspot offers, Google offers valuable and free help. Through the Adwords keyword planner it is possible to know the search volume for the keyword that has been identified as being of interest for the target audience. Google Trends, on the other hand, allows you to measure the degree of interest of that keyword in a given period, thus knowing its variations, noticing any new trends.

However, the choice of specific topics to be treated is a step subsequent to numerous others that precede it. It will be essential to first establish what the goals of our marketing action are and which target we would like to talk to. Subsequently it will be necessary to identify a message that differentiates us from the competition and that can be the beacon of our communication. Then, thoroughly analyze the market and competitors and identify the most suitable channels to spread our messages. Finally, establish what KPIs to measure to be aware of the progress of our strategy.

Defining the goals for your content strategy in the most effective way

A content strategist is called upon to confront the objectives indicated by the companies for which he works. Often, these milestones are rather vague, complicated to quantify.

"I would like to have more visibility". Would it mean having more visitors to your site? Or, "I would like to increase sales". Ok, but on which segments? Not having a magic strategy that works for everything, you need to choose which categories of people to focus your communication on to try to increase sales in that specific area. It is therefore necessary to discuss and define the goals in advance in a precise and specific way. It is on the basis of them, moreover, that each individual content and the entire content strategy must be oriented.

For example, "increasing sales generated from the youngest portion of our clients" could be a clear, concrete, measurable goal and referred to a specific target.

But what are the most common goals that a content strategy can aim to achieve? Here is an exhaustive list, that will give you a better idea on where to focus your attention.

• **Lead generation.** Contents and landing pages structured in such a way as to facilitate the compilation of a form through which to obtain useful information on potential customers.

• **Media and digital pr.** Our goal will be to obtain media coverage by creating news that has an organic, viral diffusion.

• **Distinctive positioning**. Our purpose will be defined by communicating what exactly the company does, positioning it precisely in that sector and distinguishing it from its competitors. This is an extremely important goal that, if achieved can lead to enormous amount of success.

• **Customer support.** Our contents will be aimed at clarifying the terms and conditions of the service, the characteristics of the products and the sales mechanisms.

• **Community building.** Our editorial plan will be

aimed at creating a sense of belonging, identification towards the brand through a sharing of values that emerges from a story that is as shared as possible, horizontal, friendly.

The definition of the target of a content strategy: the buyer persona

As discussed in the previous chapter, identifying the correct buyer persona is extremely important in a social media marketing strategy.

Mapping the purchasing process and intervening at every stage with the right content, at the right time, aimed at the right person is the overall and final goal of a well rounded content strategy.

To understand if a message is interesting or not, if a content can be relevant or not, we will have to understand who should receive it. Have in mind who to turn to at every time, as this is a crucial part of every social media marketing strategy.

Identifying your audience, defining it as specifically as possible is the key to drawing up a winning content strategy. Information such as age, gender, educational qualification, for many product categories are now superfluous.

At all levels of marketing, a fall in the importance of personal data is being observed in favor of buyer personas. The modern identity of the potential customer we address is reconstructed by integrating demographic and, above all, psychographic data. This means taking into strong consideration interests, behaviors, reasons for purchasing, doubts and fears regarding our service, product or our entire industry.

In short, information that is not only useful but essential to understand in which contexts these categories of people are more accessible and inclined to listen to our message and what makes that message relevant for them. We will have a dedicated chapter on this topic later on in this book.

Identify the differential message of the content strategy

Differentiate to qualify, that is key. A winning content strategy cannot ignore the identification of a differential message, of a corporate plus value that allows us to stand out from the competition. Our differential message will be our beacon. In fact, in all our content we will have to ask ourselves if it has been underlined, or at least implied. And it must be one and only one. The customer is bombarded with numerous advertisements every time he logs in and is looking for someone who can simplify his choice by clarifying which is the best, or most immediate, for that need he wants to satisfy.

It is not enough to position yourself only for the characteristics of your product

It is necessary that these are also sought after by the market and that they are not already totally controlled by the competition. In other words, you have to trigger a need and the inability to satisfy it by your competitor. That is how you win in business.

Positioning yourself on the market for a certain category or quality allows you to differentiate yourself from others

The entire content strategy will be defined by always referring to the added value that we guarantee and will aim to associate the brand with that distinctive feature that allows the simplest and most immediate mental association possible for the final consumer.

Market and competition analysis

We know we want to differentiate ourselves, but how can we do it if we do not have full and precise knowledge of what our competitors are doing?

Content strategy is still marketing, and marketing needs a benchmark. A comparative analysis with respect to our direct competitors is essential to trace the differences, their respective weaknesses and strengths. Without forgetting a broader investigation than what other similar companies do but outside our specific market, in order to obtain some useful ideas to integrate our content marketing plan.

Multi-channel content strategy

A multi-channel content strategy is essential. Stories and contents on the internet can branch out expanding, wandering, deepening, even through hypertext links. They can migrate between multiple platforms, channels, also passing from online to offline and vice versa. Our final consumer himself is now multi-channel, therefore multiplying the possibilities of intercepting him can only be one of our primary objectives.

We will have to do this by taking into account that each channel has its own characteristics that define it, peculiarities that must be taken into account already in the strategy definition phase, devising contents that can intercept and engage the audience that uses them.

What works for Facebook will most likely not work for LinkedIn, or Twitter and vice versa. The people reached will be different, the communication model adopted on the different platforms will be different. Ignoring this aspect and republishing the same content on each different digital channel can only condemn our editorial plan to irrelevance.

Organic share and promoted content

A good web content editor knows he has to follow the guides provided by the content strategist on the creation and dissemination of his contents. It will also be essential, already in the drafting phase of the strategy, to define a budget to be allocated to sponsored content. Entrusting your editorial calendar to organic distribution alone could be very limiting.

Social advertising allows us to define with extreme precision the audience we can hit. Furthermore, knowing right from the start on which categories of content to invest in order to guarantee them the necessary "push" to establish themselves and get closer to our business objectives simplifies and simplifies processes.

Chapter 11

Content Strategies for Buyer Personas

In previous chapters we have discussed the importance of having a good content strategy. We have also touched on the point that there is not a better content in absolute terms, but that it depends on who consumes said content. Let's dive a bit deeper in this concept.

Creating customized content for different buyer personas is essential to engage different consumer or user groups. David Meerman Scott gives the example of the creation of a university site that must address buyer personas with very different characteristics, objectives and motivations. In this case, the site must contain pages with content suited to the needs and expectations of the various interested parties.

Demonstrating how the creation of content can vary within the same site, the expert illustrates five possible buyer personas to be developed: former students, who are contacted to convince them to make donations; high school students, worried about submitting an application for university access and who need clear and detailed information; the parents of prospective students, who will certainly look for reassuring information on where the off-site students will live; current students to be persuaded to enroll again in a master's or other course of study; a more general section with the most frequently asked questions to avoid wasting time in university offices.

Different people come to the site or shop for different reasons, they are used to a different language and expect to find a certain type of information or certain products, which is why marketers, as explained by the expert, should undertake to use the information on buyer personas to create specific marketing and PR plans to reach each one of them.

Chapter 12

Facebook:
a Basic Introduction

Facebook Marketing is a complex topic that encompasses different functionalities, strategies, tools and features for each company and type of business. In this section, we are going to discuss every aspect there is to know to turn your Facebook page into a money making machine.

Whether you are a small local merchant, a restaurant or store, a multinational brand, on Facebook you will find tools that can help you improve your visibility, build a community, increase the awareness of your brand and the sales of your product or service, online and offline.

Facebook Marketing is a constantly evolving topic. In fact, the social media constantly updates the tools made available to companies, adding new features and expanding its capabilities.

Facebook in the US is now known and used by almost 300 million people, so it is useless to explain what the functionalities of a basic profile are, we know them very well and this book is all about giving you the most valuable information.

What no many people know and what we are going to focus on, instead, is the importance that Facebook has assumed as the best social media marketing and social e-commerce platform in the entire world.

In this section we will address the main topics of facebook marketing. You will discover the bases for a successful social media strategy. You will learn how to do facebook marketing and how to use social marketing to increase your facebook business by managing facebook fan pages and facebook ads.
Finally, we will offer you some examples of facebook social media marketing, reporting the success stories

of the best brands present online. Finally, you will have all the basic information to build your winning Facebook marketing strategies and be able to plan your social media manager training in the most effective way, if this is the route you want to take.

To start making the most of this social network by promoting your website or blog and increasing your online business, it is essential to define the goal we want to achieve. These can be:

- Promote our Brand (brand awareness)
- Build a user base
- Increase visits to the site or to individual blog articles
- Promote the sale of a product or service
- Provide a stellar customer service

Once the goals have been defined, it will be useful to create a Facebook company profile or public profile that allows a relationship between company and user.

First of all, this will be useful because you can start the dialogue with your fans, users and potential customers. Furthermore, you will then be able to use paid advertising to monetize this first audience even further.

Let's start by understanding the difference between a company page and a personal profile. When we are talking about a business page, users can decide to become followers of the company but not "friends" as happens by sending a request from a private profile.
Fans will be able to comment and express appreciation for the links and share them with their friends, creating a viral marketing mechanism. However, it will then be necessary to profile users based on interests, in fact the facebook page could reach thousands of fans but not all of them interested in the proposed contents.

So, what should you use? No matter if you have a personal brand or a multinational company. If you want to use Facebook in a professional way, always choose a business page over a personal profile. In fact, you will not be able to run ads on a personal profile, which is a big disadvantage.

Before understanding how Facebook Marketing works, let's try to explain the main fundamentals and some key concepts that characterize this social network.

Network of friendship

Facebook is based on developing and maintaining its network of online friendships. To contact a person you would like to be part of your network, you need to send a friend request. It is easily done via a button called Add to friends. In this way, you will be able to get in touch with another registered person like you: think of an old school friend you haven't seen in a long time that you found in the search engine once you have typed in his name and surname.

Likes and comments

The like key is undoubtedly, together with the comments key, one of the most popular functions of Facebook. The thumbs up expresses appreciation for a post, a photo, opinion and video on Facebook, thus allowing interaction. By clicking on the comments button users can publish your opinion on a content and make it visible to others.

Sharing

Thanks to this feature it is possible to share the contents of a page you follow, the update of personal status or of your contact, a video, a photo that you think are also interesting for other people. If you can get a lot of people to share your company posts, you are doing very well.

Notifications

The notification is that red square to report a new update, message and contact request. If you can manage to appear in the notification section of your potential clients, you are in a great position as you will surely catch their attention.

Status update

At the top of the profile home you can write a personal status that you want to share with your friends or fans. This is an important feature to share content with your audience and it is where most of your content strategy should take place.

Tag

It is a mention that a contact makes of another through a text that shows the exact name and surname of the person tagged. You can be mentioned on a photo or in a post and the recipient is notified by a notification. Tagging brands you will collaborate with is a great strategy to create a virtuous cycle of engagement.

Chat

Thanks to the chat two contacts can exchange unlimited messages in private mode. You can do this quickly by clicking on the message icon at the top, select the person and start a conversation. Thanks to the Facebook Messenger application you can do it easily even via your mobile phone. It has been more and more common to use chatbot in a social media marketing strategy to communicate directly with your potential customers.

Now that we have discussed the very basic concept of Facebook, it is time to see how you can use it to actively increase your brand exposure and reach more potential customers. We will start by taking a look at how to properly structure a business page.

Chapter 13

How to Correctly Structure a Facebook Page for your Business or Personal Brand

Now that we have learned about the basics of Facebook, it is time to take a look at how to correctly set up a business page. This is a crucial step, as it will allow you to run paid ads to your page, creating engagement with your target audience and helping your brand to get noticed. Let's see how to set up the page.

The first thing you need to know is that the creation of

a Facebook page can be done directly through the official website of the social network or through the Facebook application available for free on smartphones and tablets.

In both cases, all you need to create a Facebook page is a personal profile on the well-known social network platform, as to proceed with the creation of a Facebook page the first thing you will have to do is log in to Facebook with your profile to then follow the instructions we are about to give you step by step.

You must also know that Facebook pages are created and managed by administrators. Administrators are nothing more than people in charge of proceeding with the creation and management of a company page in all of its aspects. In essence, therefore, if you have been instructed by your company to carry out this operation, you will need to keep in mind that the company Facebook page must be created and managed through your personal account.

Do not worry, your private information, such as your name, surname or email address, will not be displayed on the Facebook page created. In essence, you can have as many pages as you want, without other people knowing you are the administrator.

Having clarified these fundamental issues, let's get to the heart of the matter. To create a Facebook page, after logging into your profile, go to the official Facebook for Business website and press the "Create a page" button that you can see in the top right corner.

Once you click on the Create a Page button, you will be redirected to the initial section dedicated to creating a Facebook page. You will then have to choose the Company or brand option, by clicking on the relevant Start button, and follow the instructions on the screen to complete the procedure for creating your page.

You must therefore type the name of the page and the category to which it belongs in the text fields that are proposed to you. To indicate the category (e.g. website or retail company), you need to start typing a term and then select one of the suggestions that appear below. When completed, click on the "Continue" button to go on.

Now choose whether to upload a profile picture for the page (by clicking on the appropriate button) or whether to skip the step. Then repeat the same operation for the cover image and that's it. You will be automatically redirected to the main section of your new page, through which you can manage all the contents of the same. We will discuss what kind of images to use on your brand's social pages in a later chapter. If you are following along, you can skip this step for now.

To make your page more complete, you need to enter all the information related to it. Click the button under the cover image, select the Edit page information item from the menu that opens and fill out the form that is proposed to you with information such as telephone number, reference website, position geographical etc.

Remember that the more complete your page profile is, the more reliability you will communicate to your audience.

We recommend creating all your pages using a laptop, as it is much easier and faster. However, you can do this using your smartphone or tablet as well. In this case, things are a little different. Here is how to do it.

How to create a Facebook page using the Facebook app

If you want to create a company Facebook page from mobile devices, you must install the official Facebook application for Android, iOS or Windows 10 Mobile. If you don't know how to do it, read my guide dedicated to the topic.

Once installation is complete, log into your account and press the ☰ button (which is located at the bottom right on iOS and at the top right on Android). Then select the item Pages from the screen that opens, press the + Create button (on Android) or the Create a page item (on iOS) and press the Start button.

Now, type the name you want to assign to your page in the appropriate text field, press the "Next" button and select a category from the appropriate drop-down menu (e.g. Brand and products or local businesses), then a subcategory from the menu that appears at the bottom and press the "Next" button again.

In the screen that appears later, type the address of the website referring to the page and click "Next". If you do not want to enter any website, tap on the "Skip" button located at the top right of your screen. Finally, choose whether to add a profile picture and a cover image for the page and, if so, select a photo from your device. Alternatively, press the "Skip" button to bypass the procedure. You can change the profile picture and the cover image at any time.

The game is done! Now press the "Visit the page" button to view your page and follow the advice you find in the Basic Elements box for the new Pages to add all the information relating to the latter.

To view the complete list of information that can be entered on the page and fill in the appropriate forms, scroll through the tabs located under the buttons for publishing content, choose the "Information" tab and tap on the "Edit information" button on the page that appears at the bottom of your screen.

Chapter 14

Choose the Best Images for your Facebook Page

If you think that the Facebook cover image is just a simple photo to embellish your page, you are wrong. This image can in fact represent a spring-board for your brand or for your company, even more so now that the new page layout announced by Facebook will give greater visibility to the creativity and message placed in this section.

The cover image is the perfect space to tell those who visit your profile something more about your brand and your products, but above all it is the perfect space to encourage a call-to-action, which can be a purchase on your ecommerce, a visit to your physical store or a phone call for a quote request.

To improve the effectiveness of your company Facebook page, first try to follow these small technical tips:

- Make sure the image dimensions are correct. The old Facebook pages required an image of 851 pixels wide and 315 pixels high; the new ones with 2021 layout require images 1014 pixels × 384 px;
- Use visual or textual elements that focus attention;
- Make your cover image an integral part of your marketing strategy;
- Upload new images on a constant basis and use the space to highlight news, promotions and initiatives of your business (giveaways, events, new products);
- Update (or try to) your cover at least once a month;
- Use the visual element to answer the visitor's hypothetical question "why should I like this page?".

This list, in addition to being already useful, can however be supplemented by 12 other creative ways to use the cover image of your Facebook page to make what you do, your company or your products, more visible and attractive.

So let's dive deeper into this topic and discover everything there is to know about choosing the perfect image for your Facebook page.

1) Inspire customers to buy your products

Surely you know how videos are very useful tools to explain to people how to take advantage of a product or service.
The same opportunity can be exploited through photos.

In fact, when you showcase what you do in your cover image, you are planting ideas in the minds of your potential customers, which could lead them to contact you to buy your product or choose your service.

In its cover image, Edible Arrangements (a company specialized in fruit compositions for events) has put its product at the center and at the forefront with a "happy birthday" message in the background, to highlight how its products are a great idea good for a gift or for decorations for a birthday party.

It's a very subtle tactic, but you can use it to portray your brand by stating "my product is something special" or "my product may be what you are looking for to give something special".

2) Show off what you do

Are you able to explain what your company does in just a second?

One of the best ways to spice up your cover image is to come up with creative ideas to advertise what you do in a way that informs people who find your brand on Facebook at a glance.

This is exactly what EYStudios (an eCommerce design company) did with its new cover image: a sharp and impactful photo that undoubtedly shows who the company is and what it does.

3) Express your personality

Visual content is a very important part of your marke-

ting and is the best way to show who you are and what personality is behind your work.
The cover of the company Facebook page is the perfect showcase to insert an image in line with the message that the company wants to convey beyond Facebook.

MailChimp, for example, uses his photo to show who the company is and his personality, using empty spaces to highlight the main subject of the photo, in order to attract all attention to it.

4) Appeal to the senses
Companies in the food sector have the opportunity to capture attention by using tempting photos of their products so as to make the observer's mouth water.
These companies have the ability to update the cover image very often both to highlight what the menu offers and to highlight any promotions.

The cover of the Facebook business page of Little Caesars (the third largest pizza chain in the US) is a blatant example of this tactic.

Papa John's (another major company in the sector)

followed the same path by highlighting the product with the promotion of the moment, while also leaving some space to underline its relationship with the Major League of Baseball.

If you are aware of the fact that your customers have specific preferences regarding some of your products, you can use this information to appeal to customers even more.

This is what the Olive Garden chain of restaurants has done. Since the company is aware that the most popular products are breadsticks and huge salads, it showed them in the foreground in the cover image and photographed them so closely that it almost seems to be sitting at the table. Cruel, but effective.

5) Contact a circle of users

For specific product companies, the Facebook cover image is the perfect way to represent not only new and upcoming products but also the latest promotions.
To maximize the impact, it is certainly effective to insert a compelling reproduction of the product, information on it, release dates in stores and "call to ac-

tion".

Logitech G, a PC accessories company, used its cover image to promote a specific product line.

The company took advantage of the space to emphasize its link with the ESL (Internet Sports League) to promote products for players.

6) Inspire creativity

Your Facebook cover doesn't always have to be the place for notifications and promotions. Often the message you want to send can get through more effectively if creativity takes over.

Take a cue from the Toys "R" Us, a children related product company. The company has in fact used a photo that recalls both adults and children to play and imagination. Fun can sometimes come from the simplest of things.

7) Promote your hashtag

Hashtags are powerful marketing tools, as we have discussed in the introductory chapter to Facebook.

Many companies have had great success using them in marketing strategies, since with hashtags they have been able to monitor what users said about their products to improve them.

Give hashtags plenty of space on your cover image to ensure as much exposure as possible, as did Calvin Klein and Monster Energy.

By taking advantage of the Facebook page cover image to highlight your hashtags for each of your advertising campaigns, people will often start looking at your image in search of promotions and alerts.

8) Value your fans

To celebrate its 100th birthday, Oreo released a new cover image showing fans on their birthday.

Customers love being part of the brand's history. If you involve your fans you will make them feel valued, you will show authenticity and humanity as integral values of your company.

Red Bull is a leader in doing this: it loves inserting user-created content in its social media pages.

9) Play on emotions

Emotions play a fundamental role in how users will

react to a product; the sensations that your products generate will therefore have a big impact.

Your cover image must exude emotions since it is these that guide decisions, changes of opinion, user requests.
Emotions are the best tool for strengthening customers' bond with a brand.

David's Bridal (a brand specializing in wedding planning) plays on the powerful emotions of couples, focusing especially on brides.
What it paints with her cover image is a scenario that generates emotion in the audience: it's the big day, you're married, the stress of the preparations is over and everything is perfect as you always dreamed.

Think back to the first time you went to the zoo. Each animal was a surprising discovery.
The Detroit Zoo through its cover image wants to remind you of that feeling and wants you to dive back into that memory.

The cover image of Parent Magazine, on the other

hand, generates emotions related to being a parent with the aim of making readers feel almost understood. It is in fact a photo that makes people exclaim: "Parent Magazine knows what it means to be parents!"

10) Promote what your target audience likes
Companies that previously limited themselves to selling products, today attract customers with extensions of their businesses: entertainment, workshops, social experiments and much more.
Companies can therefore benefit greatly from promoting their products on Facebook. But it doesn't stop there.

Think about how your customers use your products or services and what part of those products remain most impressed.
Turn everything into a visual experience and insert it at the top of your Facebook page so that your followers will want to try it.

Great Wolf Lodge (a company specialized in water parks) is one example.
Of course, showing some nice photos of their water

park would already have been effective, but showing the image of the giant water funnel is certainly more impactful.

Would you like to try it, right?

Polaris sells vehicles suitable for all types of terrain. The company knows very well how its products are actually used. It is crucial to know how your customers use your products and services.

11) Promote giveaways

There are many ways to notify your followers when you are about to start a giveaway. You can use push notifications, emails, flyers or simple word of mouth. However, many of these methods only reach those who already follow you.

Using the cover image instead allows you to make the content you want to advertise visible to all, especially new visitors.

KOA (a camping company), for example, is renowned for its large number of giveaways, which sometimes even include real caravans.

The cover image can therefore help visitors to always be aware of these giveaways. People like this will want to always be up to date on you.

12) Advertise your other social pages

If you want to have more followers on other social networks you need to let people know about them.

Use your Facebook cover image to let your users know that you have other social accounts so they can choose where and how to follow you!

Family-friendly comedian Batdad uses his cover image to showcase his other social channels and got enormous engagement on other platforms as well, thanks to this tactic.

As you can see, there is much more to choosing the perfect images for your Facebook page than "just choosing an image". Keep this in mind when you formulate the content strategy for your brand, as it can make or break the impact you have on your target audience.

Also, do not forget about the importance of colours.

Each brand has to have its own colours, as they are a powerful vehicle to be recognized by the targeted audience. When you choose the colours for your brand, try to think about the idea and message you want to convey. For instance, if you are in the wellness niche, focus on light colours, as they communicate purity and well-being. On the contrary, if you operate in the "make money online" niche, you would like to focus on gold-like colours, conveying a message of abundance to your potential customers.

When it comes to social media marketing, everything is done for a reason and has a goal in mind, even the profile picture of your Facebook page. Do not forget it.

Chapter 15

What to Do With a Business Facebook Page

Now that you have successfully learned how to create and correctly set up your Facebook page, it is time to discuss how to apply your content strategy in the best way possible. In this chapter, we are going to cover every tool at your disposal to make sure you maximize the power of your company Facebook page. Let's get started.

Every social media strategy on the web must combine quality content with a strategy capable of conveying the right message to the right people, at the right time. In this difficult strategic process, Facebook helps companies to advertise online, allowing them to create different, engaging content each time, capable of achieving multiple objectives, targeting them to specific targets.

Companies that want to promote online will obviously have to have a company Facebook profile. Therefore, the strategy to be adopted to convey the right message to the public will be planned. Facebook provides 10 different types of content or posts.

Here we explain in detail the differences between the 10 types of posts, with some useful tips to use them in the right way.

1. **Share a photo or video**
   You can share one or more photos, which you can also combine into an album, which will remain accessible to users within your company Facebook page. Together with the photo or post you can insert descriptive text, add emoticons with which you describe your mood, register your position in a specific place, perhaps your company headquarters, or another location if,

for example, you are attending a corporate event. Finally, in the post you can also tag a product that is relevant to your brand. The use of posts with images and videos statistically have a much greater engagement than posts with text only, so you should prefer this type of post. Whenever possible, include the link to your business website in your post. In this way you will increase visits to the site.

2. **Advertise your company**
With this method you can create sponsored posts that advertise your web page or your Facebook business page. Sponsored posts can be of various types: carousel, single image, link to the website, video and much more. The goals of the posts also may vary. You can choose whether to increase visits to the website, get more Likes on the Facebook page, increase the installations of your company app; in other words, you choose the goal and Facebook will help you achieve it. With the professional Facebook Ads Management tool, you can create effective promotions by monitoring their progress, target

and budget. We will discuss more about Facebook ads in a dedicated chapter.

3. **Create an offer**

   This feature allows you to create an offer, discount or promotion for your products. You will be able to include a special promotional code and also add conditions of sale. The promotion will include a photo, an expiration date and the remaining time. This is a very useful feature for promotions to be used on holidays or special occasions. Users can decide whether to save the offer, by receiving a notification before its expiration. This feature works seamlessly with the Facebook Showcase feature and is used by many users.

4. **Record a live video for your target audience**

   If you have a camera and have a specific message to convey, this is the perfect function for you. The tool is widely used by those who work in the entertainment and art sectors. We advise you to plan its use and use it only if you are at corporate events that deserve attention, or if you have already prepared your audience with an announcement about the live broadcast. Communicate the live video topic first, as this is going to set the stage for a proper conversation with your audience. Ask your audience questions and ask them what they would like to question you about. During the live broadcast you will be able to interact with the connected audience, who will be able to comment via streaming messages. Over the years, this has become a very important tool for small and medium size companies and we advise you to use it extensively to increase brand awareness.

5. **Receive phone calls from your customers or potential client**

With this tool you will create a post with an upper writing, a lower image and a slogan under the image. At the bottom right, the user will find a button that reads "Call now". By clicking on it from their mobile phone your audience can directly call the number you entered. This is a very useful function if the call to action you want to get is the conversion through phone calls.

6. **Receive messages**

   It is a post similar to the one listed above in point 5, except that instead of the "Call now" button, the user will find the "Send a message" button. This is a very useful new feature for companies, which may decide to invest in sponsored posts with this effective call to action. Users will feel pressured to send a private message via Facebook messenger. An instrument that is really popular nowadays.

7. **Help people find your company**

   This new type of post consists of an initial text, an image, a slogan and a button with a call to action called "Directions". By clicking on that button, the user will be directed to a map with directions to reach your company headquarters. This is a particularly interesting feature if you have a physical store that you would like to bring customers to.

8. **Create an event**

A much more attractive tool since it contains the new feature that allows you to insert a video on the cover instead of the photo. Below you will enter the name of the event, the place, the frequency, the start and end date, the details, the keywords, the tickets and the URL to get the tickets. This tool is widely used in the world of art and music, to promote concerts and national premieres. It can also be used to advertise corporate events or training courses.

9. **Write a note**

This is a special tool to use as an alternative to the standard post when you have particular concepts or content to transmit, such as poems or long texts. The tab allows you to write a bit like you do in a blog, complete with a title, anchor text, italics, bold and much more. You can include an image and even a link to your company's website.

10. **Create a product**

This is an innovative tool that allows you to insert a photo or video, the name of the product, the price, the ability to put it on sale, the description and the ability to share the product on your page. You can also choose whether to make it visible to everyone or keep it private to a select audience.

Especially if you have a digital product, showcasing it on your Facebook page will be fundamental to increase the perception of your brand and to attract new customers.

Now that you know every tool at your disposal to share your content on your Facebook page, it is time to dive deeper into the most important aspect of using Facebook in a social media marketing strategy. We are talking about Facebook ads and the next chapter will tell you all about them.

Chapter 16

Facebook Ads

Now that we have laid out the basics of Facebook for business, it is time to dive deeper into the most discussed and controversial topic regarding this social network. We are talking about the possibility to advertise, reaching potential customers and users by paying.

As always, let's start with a definition.

Defining Facebook ADS is pretty simple. It's Facebook's advertising system. ADS in fact stands for advertising, so the concept is quite clear. On how things work, things get a little more complicated, because if it is true that creating an ad is in itself a quick and painless process, creating an ad that achieves good or excellent results is pretty complex and requires a good dose of technical knowledge and experience.

But let's go step by step. Why should a company advertise on Facebook?

Given that later we will discuss in detail the specific goals that we can try to pursue thanks to Facebook ADS, in a nutshell we can now tell you that using this tool you have the possibility to propose your content or products to a group of potentially interested people; and you can do it by crossing the limit of fans of your fanpage, or by addressing a small subset of all subscribers.

Fan? fanpage? Yes, Facebook ADS is reserved for fan pages, you cannot start a campaign from your personal profile or from a group. And this explains the main reason why there is no point in trying to represent your business with anything other than a fanpage, as we have told you in previous chapters.

The reasons for the success of Facebook ADS

Why is Facebook ADS so talked about? The reason is actually very simple: it works very well. Over the course of its existence - that is, from the now distant 2011 until today - the Facebook advertising platform has undergone numerous updates, changes and second thoughts. The only aspect that has really remained unchanged is its performance. Obviously you must know how to move within the interface as well as you must necessarily know the concepts and variables that determine the success of a campaign. In this guide we will explain everything you need to know to start experimenting with this tool. The commitment and experience that you will accumulate by playing with Facebook ADS will do the rest. As for anything in life, practice makes perfect.

The structure of Facebook ADS campaigns

Regardless of the goal you choose, each Facebook ADS advertising campaign will be hierarchically structured on three distinct levels:

- **Level 1: Campaign** - In this first step you have to decide what will be the main goal that your ads will try to pursue. Once you have given a unique identifying name to the new campaign you can move on to the next level.

- **Level 2: Ad Group** - If the previous step was rather mechanical, here you will have to work more than that by defining the duration, the assigned budget and the target audience that will be reached by your ads. You will also decide on the placement and payment methods. It is important to note that a single campaign can contain multiple ad groups.

- **Level 3: Ads** - In this last step you will have to create the actual ad, or choose what users will see every time your ad is actually published on Facebook. Basically it is about creating posts by carefully choosing the copy (the portions of text that will make up the ad) and the visual (therefore images, videos or slideshows). Also in this case you must always keep in mind that a single group of advertisements can contain more than one ad.

Only three steps and yet - as we will see - the difficulties behind each of these are not to be underestimated. Knowing how to untangle this process will make the difference between a successful campaign and one that simply burns money unnecessarily. For the moment, however, let's worry about summarizing the structure of Facebook campaigns.

How to create a new Facebook ADS campaign
To create your first Facebook ADS campaign, start by clicking on the arrow found on any Facebook screen at the top right. From the drop-down menu that will be generated, press "Create ad".

As you can see we are ready to start. But first note that if you have some ad blocking extension installed on your browser (AdBlock Plus for example) you will receive an error message. To use Facebook ADS correctly, you will need to disable the blocks on Facebook domains or, alternatively, suspend the operation of the advertisement during the creation process.

The goals of Facebook ADS campaigns

As you can see, the goals available for Facebook ADS campaigns are numerous. Ten to be exact. They are all specific and each has its own unique features. All of them are perfect to meet a specific need your company or personal brand may have. However, for beginners, they can create a bit of confusion. Is it better to choose Increase conversions on your website or Drive people to your website? Better to highlight a post or promote the page? To answer these questions, we will describe each of these ten goals to you, but you too have to go all in with us to clear your mind.

Facebook Advertising must always be part of a well-defined online marketing strategy before attempting to create campaigns. We have discussed this many times when we talked about having a social media marketing strategy.

So in a certain way you should have set the goal before starting the ad creation process, this is not the moment to improvise. Now it is just a matter of putting into practice what you and your co-workers previously planned. I insist on this point because, on the contrary, most novice entrepreneurs with online marketing approach Facebook ads without adequate preparation. They think that after all it would be nice to find new customers and they throw themselves into the instrument without having clear their purposes and, in the most tragic cases, not even the nature of the medium. So always remember to plan before putting into practice!

Let's take a look at the different goals your campaign can have.

Direct people to your website
In this case, the goal of the campaign is to encourage users to click on the ad in order to view a page of your website. Once this goal has been selected, in fact, you will be asked to enter the URL of the page you want to promote.

Specify the address and you will be asked to create your Facebook Pixel. To do this, simply click on Create pixel and thanks to this Facebook will be able to optimize the performance of your campaigns. We will talk about the pixel in the next chapter. Once you have assigned a name to the new campaign, click on Create advertising account (if this is your first time in advertising on Facebook) or on Set audience and budget if you have already used Facebook ADS before.

Increase conversions on your website

In this case, the goal is to bring people to your website and, in addition, make them complete a purchase or a registration process. Conversion must therefore be interpreted with its broadest meaning, i.e. independent of the concept of sale.

To create a campaign of this type, you need to create a conversion pixel and install it correctly on the pages of your website. So, if you don't know how to create it and install it on your website, we invite you to read the next chapter, as it will explain everything you have to know about this topic.

Once the pixel has been created, you will need to specify a web address to promote and select a conversion action that signals Facebook that your goal has been achieved.

Why can't I just use the "Direct people to your website" feature?

Earlier we were talking to you about possible confusion between the various goals and now this question will probably whirl through your head. In this case and to an inexperienced eye, there could be an overlap between the two lenses. In reality this is not the case, of course. A campaign that targets conversions will choose to show ads to all people in the target audience that are similar to those who have completed a conversion in the past. While the goal of the campaign is to direct people to the website, the Facebook algorithm will look for people, among those who make up the target, particularly inclined to consult content shared on the social network. This will significantly reduce the cost of the campaign.

Make your posts stand out

With this aim, we are no longer trying to take people out of Facebook. Or at least this is not the main goal of this type of advertising. In this case we are trying to get engagement, meaning likes, comments and shares for a post that we have published on the page.

First, Facebook asks us to enter the name of the fanpage affected by the campaign or, if it is not possible to select it using the name, enter the URL of the same page. Obviously, in order to create an advertisement on behalf of a fanpage, it is necessary to have a suitable role in managing it.

After choosing the fanpage, you will be asked to indicate which post to highlight.

Increase participation in your event

If you have created an event from the manager of your fanpage and you want to ensure that potentially interested people in your area are aware of it, this is the type of campaign for you. As with the previous goals, just enter the name or address of the event to be promoted to begin the creation process.

Get people to ask for your offer

Practically the exact copy of the previous goal, but in this case we will highlight an offer. Note, however, that what is here understood as an offer is not a promotion or discount on your website, but an offer created using the appropriate publication tool on the fan pages.

Get video views

If you have published native videos on Facebook and want to increase their views, this type of campaign is ideal for achieving your goal. Also in this case a useful clarification is needed. As you can see, we specified native videos, that is, uploaded directly to Facebook. You can't use this feature to promote content posted on YouTube, Vimeo, or other video sharing platforms. In these cases, if you need to increase their visibility through Facebook ADS, you will need to create an ad hoc post on your fanpage and sponsor them using the "Highlight your posts" goal.

But what difference does it make?
As in the previous cases, here too it is a question of target audience optimization. In the case of featured posts, we seek engagement for certain types of posts. Regarding video views, Facebook will focus on selecting people who have shown particular interest in videos and perhaps who tend to see them for longer than others.

Now that we have seen the main goals you can choose from when creating a campaign, it is time to focus on the actual creation process.

Creating an advertising account

If this is your first time using Facebook ADS, after selecting the campaign goal and filling in all the required fields, you will have clicked on the "Create advertising account" button.

In the advanced settings you will be given the option to change the name of the account which, without changes, will take the name of your Facebook profile. Once we have checked that all settings are correct, we can proceed to the next step.

Ad groups

Well, now that you have selected the goal of your new campaign, Facebook wants to know other essential information: who to show your ads to, the period within the advertising campaign will be active and what your spending budget is.

In order to avoid turning the reading of this chapter into a too extreme test of mental resilience, we cannot show you the creation of ad groups and, subsequently, the ads for each different campaign seen previously. Each will have its own configuration details, but what is really important in a beginner's guide, as this one, are the general concepts and these will be addressed in great detail.

Definition of the target audience

It all starts here and believe us when we tell you that this is the most delicate step of the whole creative process. Later you will understand why, for the moment, trust us and pay a lot of attention.

We must skim and try to reduce the potential audience in order to isolate all those who might be genuinely interested in what we have to propose.

To keep track of the number of people who make up your audience and an estimate of the quality of your targeting, you will find a graph and an indication of the potential coverage of the ad group in the top right. As for the graph, always keep in mind that it is more choreographic and is able to correctly report only the extreme cases, so do not rely too much on it.

In order to select the proper audience, you have to have your buyer persona in mind. This is why it is extremely important that you do the research process described in the previous chapters, before creating your first ad. This will take a bit of time, but it will save you a lot of money.

Why don't we show the ad to everyone instead? isn't it cheaper?

No, it is a mentality that, although it might be right in some areas, is exactly the opposite of that required to be successful with Facebook Advertising. The algorithm that determines how much we will pay for achieving individual goals - in this case how much we will pay each time a user clicks on the ad and reaches the website - depends on how often the people to whom the ads are shown perform that particular action. In jargon we call it "Click Through Rate" (CTR) and it is expressed as a percentage.

If an ad is shown 100 times receiving 5 clicks, the corresponding CTR will be 5%. Although in reality the factors that come into play to determine the cost of each action are many, as an approximation we can safely assert that the "Cost Per Action" (CPA) is indirectly proportional to the CTR, so the more the percentage of people who click on the content increases, the more the CPA decreases.

Going back to the definition of the audience, you should now have clearer why it is so important. In fact, if we show our advertisement to a selected group of people so that many of them are interested, we will get a high CTR thus lowering the CPA. By maintaining an extremely large and heterogeneous audience, the CTR will inevitably plummet, sending the CPA sky high.

Why did Facebook do this devilry?
One of Facebook's goals has always been to avoid the invasion of traditional advertising on its pages. When the introduction of an advertising system became necessary to capitalize on the enormous volume of subscriptions, they set themselves the goal of programming an algorithm that would allow users to be reached only by quality content and in which they could be really interested. In this way, advertising stops being invasive and, on the contrary, can even become

useful for discovering products and services that we are not aware of.

It is a sort of transparent advertising, therefore, which in order to be realized needs the collaboration of all advertisers. Clearly we could not expect a free collaboration and this payment system has proved to be the best deterrent for the incapable advertisers, since, in addition to spending more on average, a poorly performing ad will tend to be delivered more rarely by Facebook and therefore will reach a increasingly fewer number of users at the same cost. In short: it is not convenient at all to target everyone on the planet.

Now that we understand that targeting your ad audience is very important, it's time to go into detail and see how to properly define it. Please, keep in mind that you should have a specific idea of your target before starting the ad creation process.

Demographic targeting

In the first section we can affect purely demographic parameters. The preset location is the US, but we can select any place, even the smallest villages. When a municipality is selected, Facebook allows us to establish a radius in addition to the city within which to show the ad.

By acting on the selector next to the number of kilometers, we can narrow or expand the area involved.

At the moment all people who are in the area are selected. So a passing tourist stopped at a motorway restaurant could see our ad if he uses Facebook, perhaps from a smartphone. However, we can change this type of setting by acting on the selector at the top, or on the button on which you find written "All the people in this place".

There are four possible settings:

- All people in this place: will involve everyone who access Facebook in the demarcated area for the ad group.

- People who live in this place: it will involve all users who have reported the residence within the set range of action.

- People who were recently in this place: it will involve all the people who recently passed through the selected area.

- People traveling to this place: it will involve all people whose most recent position is the selected area based on the information provided by the mobile device.

It is also important to note that, again in terms of geographical delimitation, we can include and exclude other locations. By clicking on "Include" we will open a drop-down menu from which to select the option that allows us to choose other areas to exclude and include.

Age, gender and language

After specifying the area of action of our advertising group, we can proceed by defining the age, gender and language spoken by the people interested in our advertisement. The language field is particularly important and should not be confused with the area of residence: imagine in fact that you want to offer Italian language courses. Obviously you will try to select people living in Italy who have not set Italian as their main language.

Detailed targeting

Here we go straight to the heart of targeting. Through the detailed targeting fields we can in fact specify the interests and behaviors of the people we are going to reach. If you start typing something, Facebook will take care to give you some suggestions. In any case, you will have to select the characteristics that best describe the interested public, thus delimiting the potential coverage of the ad group.

To successfully accomplish this task we can use:

- Demographics
- Interests
- Behaviors
- Other categories

To go into more detail, you can start typing and see the suggestions offered by the interface or use the Browse tab and navigate between the various categories.

Before proceeding with the creation of your campaign, we advise you to carefully browse the categories in order to realize the real potential of the tool.

Exclude people or narrow your audience

So far we have entered interests or behaviors and we have broadened the target audience. In fact, the interests indicated so far are linked through a logical disjunction, namely:

Public = Interest1 or Interest2 or Interest3 or... or Interest4

If, on the other hand, you want to restrict the audience by cutting off people you do not think may be interested, you have two features available.

- Exclude People. It allows you to select interests, behaviors or demographics in the same ways you used previously. However now you are not adding but excluding people who match the selected characteristics. If you add more than one, a user just needs to meet at least one of the listed criteria to be excluded.

- Narrow the audience. Again you will select the interested audience by indicating the characteristics as done previously. However, now you are asking Facebook's algorithm to compose the audience so that, in addition to all the other characteristics, users also satisfy at least one of those indicated here.

Please note that you are not obliged to use all the targeting possibilities offered. However, especially by keeping in mind what has been said about the relationship between CTR and CPA, we invite you to think carefully when you are going to create your audiences in order to make the best possible use of the tools you have available.

The connections

To complete the definition of the target audience for your new Facebook Ads campaign, only the last piece is missing: connections. Thanks to these, you can further define your selection by adding or excluding people based on how they previously came in contact with your online business.

Connections allow you to target based on different types of actions they have performed so far. In detail:

Facebook pages
- People who like your page
- Friends of people who like your page
- Exclude people who like your page

Applications
- People who have used your application
- Friends of people who have used your application
- Exclude people who have used your application

Events
- People who responded to your event
- Friends of the people who responded to your event
- Exclude people who have already responded to your event

Therefore, supposing you want to create a new campaign to increase the likes of your company's fanpage, obviously you will want to exclude people who already like your page so as not to show your ad unnecessarily and thus trigger the usual vicious circle between CTR and CPA.

If you notice using this type of selection it is not possible for you to intersect the various results. For example, you can't target everyone who has used your application while excluding people who are fans of your page. To build this type of conditions you have to select "Advanced combinations" from the connections menu.

Once this step is also completed, you can decide to save the audience thus generated by checking the "Save this audience" box or proceed further and define the budget.

Budget definition

How much to spend on Facebook depends more on your pocket than on the tool itself. Usually the biggest risk entrepreneurs run is having a big budget and squandering it on poorly optimized campaigns. In fact, net of macroscopic errors, by investing so much money, the results tend to arrive even working in a rough way.

Clearly they would arrive more abundant if the campaign were professionally managed, but often one does not realize how many opportunities are being squandered, dazzled by the results that still continue to arrive.

My advice, therefore, is to start by investing a modest amount in relation to the total budget. Test different things using different target audiences and different types of advertisements. When you have identified the best performing combinations, push the accelerator and invest more money on them.

Daily budget and total budget

The first choice you need to make is to specify to Facebook how much money you want to invest in the campaign. You have two options:

- Daily budget. You are communicating to Facebook the amount you are willing to invest every day for your campaign. By using this type of budget you can avoid setting the date on which the campaign will end and therefore it will be up to you to deactivate it when you see fit.

- Total budget. In this case you set the total amount of expenditure that you are willing to incur. By selecting this mode you will be asked to set a start date and the date on which the campaign will end. It will be the Facebook algorithms to determine how to distribute the expenditure over the indicated period.

Which to use?

The criticism that is most often heard about the daily budget is that it tends to spend the expected money in any case, even at the cost of delivering the ad to that part of your target audience that rarely performs the action you are trying to achieve. To verify that this widespread belief was true, we tried to conduct a test by creating two identical campaigns in everything apart from the budget breakdown.

In one case we left the daily budget, in the other we set the total budget so that the subdivision of this along the duration would lead us to have a daily distribution identical to the daily budget set in the first case. Obviously, several factors may have intervened to change the performance of the two campaigns, but the total budget actually spent different figures depending on the days, leaving us to imagine a better optimization in the delivery of the advertisements.

On the other hand, the total budget generally requires a higher minimum investment threshold - at least five dollars per day - than can be set using the daily budget. In some cases we have created campaigns which, spending just 2 dollars per day, have still brought excellent results to the customer. To run them we necessarily had to use the daily budget, though.

Once these settings have been completed, we are ready to move on to the next step, which is the creation of the advertisements. Being a guide reserved for beginners, we do not dwell on the advanced options that you find immediately under the box we have just discussed. For now, just know that in the vast majority of cases the default settings are perfect.

Creating your Ads

We have finally arrived at the last, fundamental step in the construction of a new Facebook ads campaign: we are about to create an ad.

It is a very important step because, after having carefully defined who will be the target of our advertising activity, we now have to create the elements that will actually come into contact with the public. It is therefore natural that we will have to pay particular attention to all the characterizing aspects of the advertisements.

Now is the moment where the content strategy comes into play. If you don't have one yet, we suggest you read the previous chapters again before proceeding.

The first choice you can make is the ability to create a new ad or use an existing post and promote that. If the goal of the campaign is different from the promotion of a post, it is advisable to proceed with the creation of a new advertisement. The posts you publish on your fanpage are hardly optimized to perform at their best in an advertising campaign.

Standard or carousel listings

Proceeding with the creation of a new advertisement you will have to choose which format to use. You can select between only an image or a video in your advertisements (standard advertisements) or multiple images in an advertisement (carousel advertisements)

The substantial difference lies in the presentation of the visual, or the creative content present in the advertisement. In the first case, the image has a 16: 9 form factor and at the same time you have more space for the title and description of the content you are sharing. In the second one you can upload up to a maximum of five square images (1:1 ratio) which can then be browsed by pressing the side arrows. You will increase the visual impact while sacrificing space for the title and description.

Note that every single image of a carousel advertisement can direct the user to a specific address, so they are particularly effective advertisements if you want to promote e-commerce products. Also keep in mind that this format usually allows you to achieve generally better results in terms of CTR than traditional ads. This however does not mean that you will always have to use carousels anyway, as it all depends on your target audience. So our advice is - as always - to test and figure out which ads give the best results to your specific company or personal brand.

Creating an advertisement

Once you have selected the format of the new advertisement, you can proceed to its composition. In this case, let's see how to create a carousel since the process is slightly more complex and in any case allows us to also illustrate all the steps necessary to create a standard ad.

Link a page

First select a page to link to the ad you are creating. In this way, any interactions gained from the ad will increase the engagement of the selected page. Clearly you should select the page that represents the business you are promoting.

Create a copy

The next step is to create a copy. Depending on the type of campaign you have selected, you will have more or less characters available, in any case Facebook will inform you when you reach the maximum threshold.

Order of carousels and information card

If you have filled in the copy textbox, now you need to consider the two options related to images and links.

The first option (Automatically show first the links and images that get better results) allows Facebook algorithms to change the order of appearance of the images of the carousel ads in order to put in the first positions those with the best performance, that is, in the case of this specific campaign, those with the highest CTR.

The second option, on the other hand, allows you to decide whether to include an additional card reserved for your brand in your new carousel. It will therefore be a generic post that will show the profile image of the linked fanpage and a web address of your choice.

Visual and descriptions

Now it's time to create the visual part of the ad. As you can see, you have a selector at your disposal with which you can select each single slot that makes up the listing. For each of these you can select an image, a title, a description (this is the only optional field) and a destination URL.

In case you need more slots than the three open by default you will have to press the "+" button. As mentioned above, the maximum limit is five slots.

When creating the image for your ads, it is important to follow the former 20% rule, which states not to occupy more than 20% of the image with text.

The concept is very simple: Facebook prefers images to be images, not blocks of graphical text. So you can't cover the creatives you attach to your Facebook ADSs with promotional copy. At one time (until about a year ago) the 20% rule was in force, according to which the text could not cover more than twenty percent of the total surface of the image. It wasn't that easy to do the calculations by eye, and the verification tool sometimes did not work properly. It is suffice to say that once the limit was exceeded, the ad was rejected.

Recently Facebook replaced the old rule with a new

mechanism.

For all images containing text for an area of less than 20% of the total, there are still no problems. For surpluses we no longer have the automatic rejection, but we have a progressive decrease in the potential reach with a consequent and inevitable increase in CPM. It is up to you to assess whether it can be convenient and whether any increase in performance is able to repay you for this initial gap.

There are many online tools that can evaluate the ratio between text and picture in your image. We recommend that you use them and still respect the old 20% rule for maximum results.

Call to action button

It seems like a trifle, but the call-to-action button is often able to significantly increase the CTR of your campaign. It is therefore a good practice to always select one whenever possible. The options that Facebook gives us for this ad element are the following.

- No buttons

- Buy now
- Book now
- Find out more
- Subscribe
- Download
- See more
- Request now
- Contact us

Whatever your choice, know that the button will direct the user to the address provided by the specific tab (in the case of carousel advertisements) or by the entire advertisement (in the case of a standard advertisement).

Preview and placement

As you have surely noticed during the entire creation phase, the Facebook ads interface creates a dynamic preview of the ad on the right side of the screen.

From this module, we can see the selected placements for our ads. These are the following.

- Computer News section. This ad format will be

shown on the News Feed (the list of all posts) of target users who view Facebook using a personal computer

- News section of mobile devices. This format is reserved for target users who view their News Feed using smartphones or tablets

- Right column of computers. This format generates ads that will compose the right column that usually appears on every Facebook page. This format does not display the ads on mobile.

- Audience Network. This format allows you to occupy positions on mobile apps and websites that use the Facebook advertising network. In other words, your ads will appear outside the usual context of the social network

- Instagram. One of the latest Facebook ADS introductions. As you probably already know, Instagram is property of Facebook and for a few months now it has also been possible to take advantage of the most popular photo-centered social network in the world.

Check the previews and optimize the ads

First, always remember, to check the previews for any Facebook ads placements you decide to activate. Unfortunately, the length of the text portions is different for each format so you may end up with a perfect ad for the News Section on your computer but that performs poorly on mobile devices.

If your campaign has a high budget, you can consider the idea of creating specific ad groups for the various placements. If, on the other hand, you have to deal with a tight budget, it may not make sense to segment it further (remember that you must reserve a part of the budget for each group of ads) and therefore you will have to try to mediate between the characteristics of the various placements that you decide enable.

Which placements to enable?

Normally we recommend that you enable all of them and leave the performance statistics to judge the goodness of a placement. Much depends on the subject matter and the type of campaign you are creating. Facebook ADS is always ready to amaze you. On more than one occasion we have had unexpected results from the most unlikely placements (obviously unlikely according to our expectations).

It is therefore an excellent habit to never preclude yourself from any feature. The first few days of the campaign will serve you to fine-tune it and fix all the small imperfections that will inevitably crop up. Once the statistics highlight the less performing placements you can disable them and stick with what is performing.

We have finally finished the process of creating your new campaign. All you have to do is click on the "Order" button in order to submit it to the Facebook ADS team for approval. If you have done everything correctly this will arrive to them in a few minutes and in the following hours the advertisements will start to be displayed to the selected audience.

Chapter 17

Facebook Pixel

At the beginning of the previous chapter, we have briefly talked about Facebook Pixel and how important it is to use it properly in order to maximize the impact of your campaigns. Let's dive a bit deeper and discover a bit more about it.

As always, let's start with a definition.

The Facebook pixel is a snippet of code that you can place on your website. It will collect the data with which you can measure conversions from your Facebook ads, optimize them, create your target audience for future campaigns and retarget users who have already performed an action on your website.

It works by activating cookies that have the task of monitoring user interactions on your website and in your Facebook ads.

In the past, there were two different types of Facebook pixels: the conversion pixel and the custom audience pixel. The former was abandoned by Facebook in 2017. Even if you used it in the past, now you have to switch to the new one. As this is a book for beginners, we assume you have no previous experience, so you are not affected by this change.

Why should you use the Facebook pixel?
The Facebook pixel gives you useful information to create more effective Facebook ads, targeting a personalized audience. With the data obtained from the Facebook pixel measurements, you always have the certainty that your ads are seen by people who, in all probability, will perform the action you want. This allows you to improve the conversion rate of your Facebook ads and get a higher ROI from social networks.
Not using Facebook Ads for your social media marketing strategy yet? Our advice is to install the Facebook pixel anyway right now. That way, you can start collec-

ting the data you need right away when you're ready to create your first sponsored ad on Facebook.

Here are some ideas to make the most of the pixel and improve the results of your Facebook marketing campaigns.

Use Facebook Conversion Tracking

The Facebook pixel allows you to follow user interactions on your website after they have viewed your ad on Facebook.

You can even track customers across all of their devices. So you will be able to understand if they prefer to view your ads on mobile and perhaps switch to the desktop at the time of purchase. This information can help you refine your advertising strategy and calculate your return on investment in a much more accurate way.

Use Facebook retargeting

Facebook pixel retargeting data and dynamic ads allow you to show personalized ads to people who have already visited your site. And here you can be really precise. For example, you can show the ad of the specific product that the person in question had abandoned in the cart or added to the wish list on your website.

Create similar audiences

Facebook is able to use its targeting data to help you build an audience of people with similar tastes, interests and ages to those of the audience already interacting with your website. This way, you can broaden your potential customer base.

Optimize Facebook Ads for Conversions

Without a pixel, the only conversions you can optimize for are link clicks. The pixel, on the other hand, allows you to optimize your ads for conversions more akin to your business goals, such as purchases and subscriptions.

Optimize Facebook ads for value

By collecting data on who buys your products or services and how much they spend on your website, Facebook can optimize the audience of your ads based on its value. In other words, your ads will automatically be shown to those most likely to make higher-value purchases.

Get more tools and metrics

Do you want to use conversion campaigns on the web, custom audiences from your site or dynamic ads? All this is only possible if you install the Facebook pixel. The pixel can also be useful in measuring metrics such as cost per lead or cost per conversion.

How to use the Facebook pixel

You can use the Facebook pixel to collect data relating to two types of events. Facebook has predefined a series of 17 standard events, but you can always set up your own custom events.

An "event" is nothing more than a specific action performed by a visitor on your website. For example, making a purchase.

Facebook Pixel Standard Events

The 17 Facebook pixel standard events for which just copy and paste the standard event code are the following.

1. Buy: When someone completes a purchase on your website.

2. Lead: When someone signs up for a trial or otherwise identifies themselves as a contact on your website.

3. Complete registration: when someone completes a registration form on your website, such as a registration.

4. Add payment info: when someone enters their payment details during the purchase process on your website.

5. Add to Cart: When someone adds a product to their cart on your website.

6. Add to wishlist: When someone adds a product to the wishlist on your website.

7. Start Checkout: When someone initiates the process of going to checkout during a purchase on your website.

8. Search: When someone uses the Search feature to find an article on your site.

9. View Content: When someone lands on a specific page on your website.

10. Contact us: when someone contacts your business.

11. Personalize the product: when someone selects a specific version of the product, for example a certain color.

12. Donate: When someone makes a donation to your cause.

13. Find position: when someone searches for the physical location of your company.

14. Schedule: When someone books an appointment at your company.

15. Start Trial: When someone signs up to try your

product for free.

16. Submit Request: When someone requests your specific product, service or program, such as a credit card.

17. Subscribe: When someone subscribes to a paid product or service.

Additional details can be added to standard events using code snippets called parameters. These allow you to customize standard events based on:

- Value of the conversion event
- Currency
- Content type or ID
- Cart contents

For example, you can use Facebook's measurement pixel to record views of a specific category on your website, rather than measuring all views across the board. Let's say you own a pet supplies website; you may want to separate dog owners from cat owners based on the sections of the site viewed and the Facebook Pixel allows you to do just that.

Facebook Pixel Custom Events

You can use custom events instead of standard ones to gather more detail than the basic ones can offer.

Custom events use URL rules based on specific URLs or URL keywords. Again, this is an extremely advanced feature that you will rarely use in your social media marketing campaign. Therefore, we have decided to leave it as it is important that you focus on the most important information first.

How to create a Facebook pixel to add to your website

Now that you know what to monitor and why, it's time to create your pixel and make it work on your website.

Step 1: create your pixel

- From your Facebook Events Manager, click on the hamburger icon (≡) at the top left and select Pixel

- Click on the green Create a Pixel button

- Give your pixel a name, type the URL of your website and click Create

When choosing the name for your pixel, remember that, with Events Manager, you only have one pixel for each ad account. The name should represent your business and not a specific campaign. If you want to use more than one pixel per ad account, you can do so with Facebook Business Manager.

Step 2: add the pixel code to your website
At this point, in order to make your pixel work and have it collect information on your website, you need to install some codes on your web pages. There are various ways to do this, depending on the web platform used.

If you use an ecommerce platform like Squarespace or a tag manager like Google Tag Manager, you can directly install your pixel without having to change your website code.

If you work with a developer or other experts who can help you edit your web code, click Email Developer Instructions to send all the information needed to install the pixel.

If none of the above cases are yours, you will need to insert the pixel code directly into your web pages. Below we will guide you step by step.

- Click on Install the code manually

- Copy and paste the pixel code into your website title code. In other words, post it after the <head> tag, but before the </head> tag. You will need to paste it on every page or in your template (if you have one).

- Decide whether to use automatic advanced matching. This option allows you to associate Facebook profiles with customer data collected on your website. This allows you to track conversions much more accurately and create larger audiences of customers.

- Check if you have correctly installed the code by entering the URL of your website and clicking on Send test traffic.

Your Facebook pixel is ready to track activities. Now click on "Continue" to go to step 3.

Step 3: Monitor the right events for your business

Choose which of the 17 standard events you want to monitor using the toggle buttons. For each event, you will have to choose between monitoring when the page is loaded or monitoring the action online. Here is the difference between the two options.

- Page loading monitoring. The feature monitors actions such as visiting a new page, placing a like on the completion of a purchase or terminating the subscription on a page.

- Online action monitoring. This feature monitors the actions performed within the page (such as clicking on the "add to cart" button), which do not open a new page.

Also, you can set parameters for certain events. For

example, in case you want to track purchases of a specific dollar value.

If you want to use Facebook Pixel Custom Events, go to your Facebook Events Manager.

Select Custom Conversions from the top left menu. Then click Create Custom Conversion to define your custom conversion event using URL rules.

Step 4: Confirm that your Facebook pixel is working properly
Previously, you tested the installation of your Facebook pixel by sending test traffic. In any case, before collecting and analyzing the data from your Facebook pixel, send confirmation of its correct functioning.

Add the Facebook Pixel Helper extension to your Google Chrome browser. (Available exclusively for Chrome; if you are using a different browser, you must install Chrome to use the Pixel Helper)
Visit the page where you installed the Facebook pixel. If the extension finds the pixel, the </> icon will turn blue and a popup will tell you how many pixels it

found on the page. The popup will also tell you if your pixel is working correctly. Otherwise, it will provide you with the error data, in order to allow you to correct it.

Step 5: Add the pixel notification to your website
As required by Facebook's terms of use (and applicable regulations), you must let your website visitors know that you are collecting their data.

In other words, you must clearly communicate that you are using the Facebook pixel and that the data could be collected through cookies or other methods. You must also let users know that they can refuse consent to the collection of data concerning them.

Please, do not overlook this last step even if your personal brand or company is relatively small. Privacy is extremely important and following these rules will give you peace of mind.

Chapter 18

The Basics of Copywriting for Social Media Marketing

Now that we have extensively covered how to create your advertising campaign on Facebook, it is important to talk about the basics of copywriting. This skill is absolutely fundamental to take your content strategy to the next level and to improve the conversion rate of your posts and articles.

Here is the definition of copywriting.

Copywriting is the activity of writing advertising texts, within the broader marketing sector, with the aim of attracting and capturing the attention of the target

The results that are intended to be achieved through advertising materials can be many, but these are always and closely linked to triggering a concrete action by the user. In most cases, this action consists in a subscription or a purchase. Those who deal with copywriting, therefore, must be salesmen, to the extent that, through the use of the right written words, they manage to persuade the customer or user to take an action. For instance, buying or even responding to a call-to- action aimed at a possible future sale, through the acquisition of a lead, or a contact.

Copywriting, therefore, is not an art - as we read in many articles on the internet- it is not to the extent that the drafting of advertising texts does not convey its own interiority and the aim to be achieved is not only that of communicating and arousing emotions. The text must promote a brand and must convey, through words, specificities such as to capture the attention of users and trigger emotions that make them remember it later, when they make a purchase or in any case take an action in favor of the brand.

Copywriting is often defined as an art because of the dose of creativity that this job requires. In fact, you cannot be a copywriter without being creative, without knowing how to play with words, with their meanings, with figures of speech, without knowing how to arouse in the mind others images and concepts, even abstract ones.

Furthermore, we cannot say that copywriting is a science or that it has such scientific rigor as to lead to certain results. Copywriting, however, is a marketing activity, for which specific knowledge and an accurate strategic and analytical study of the brand's objectives, market and target audience are required, in order to aim at achieving certain results.
Approaching "scientific copywriting" means admitting that creativity is not always everything and, indeed, sometimes it must be put aside: being creative without having a method will not lead to poor results.

The texts written by a copywriter are numerous, both offline and online.

Among the offline texts are those for:

- advertisements for magazines and newspapers or billboards, in all of their components. From the headline to the body copy, slogan or claim and payoff;
- texts on the packaging, on product packages, sometimes also containing coupons to be used for subsequent purchases and invitations to collect points;
- brochures, postcards, flyers, etc;
- television and radio commercials.

Among the online texts, there are:

- newsletters and more generally texts for email marketing activities with a sales purpose;
- product sheets on eCommerce sites;
- advertisements for online platforms;
- texts that contain calls-to-action;
- banner.

Copywriting techniques

What are the most effective copywriting techniques

when it comes to social media marketing?

Let's start with a consideration. The main task of the copywriter is to write ads capable of capturing the attention of the target audience.

As this is a work based on creativity, it is difficult to establish precise rules to guide the work. However, we can outline some guidelines.

First of all it is necessary to identify the target to be reached, because the message is effective only if it adopts a language suitable for the target audience. The more specific the audience, the easier it is to hit the goal.

Since the ultimate goal of a copywriting activity is to sell, the product must occupy a central position with respect to the creative idea. For this reason it is important to follow the principle of the Unique Selling Proposition (USP), that is the formulation of a single creative idea, which will have to highlight the characteristic considered most important when designing the strategy, following the indications of a brief.

Finally, contradictions must be avoided. In fact, it is essential that the image and the text say different things, so as not to overlap, but complementary, to complete each other's message. A well-set formal structure makes the ad easier to decode and allows you to get in tune with the target audience more quickly.

Once these basic concepts on copywriting are establi-shed, let's see together some simple techniques for creating effective and engaging content, especially on the web.

The first copywriting technique consists in repeating the title. When writing a copy you will have to repeat in the text the same words used in the title but combi-ned in a different way or enriched with the addition of further information to reinforce the message. Also in the field of Search Engine Optimization this technique is very useful for communicating important informa-tion to search engine robots.

The second technique involves concreteness. The goal in this case is to attract the reader or user by focusing on a problem or interest of the user himself. Introducing concrete and measurable data and new information compared to that offered by competitors, makes the copy really attractive to the target audience.

The "problem technique" instead consists in asking a common question, to which many users seek an answer, to make them feel involved in the discussion. But be careful, because the question must be a real question and not a rhetorical question, to which everyone already knows the answer. Otherwise the risk is to frustrate the readers.

The second to last technique is the "alternative technique". After we have posed the question using the problem technique, we can also offer a concrete answer or an alternative to an already known answer, proposing ourselves as experts in our sector. In this case it is important to highlight all the features of the product or service we offer that can help the target audience to solve their problem.

The last technique is focused on a call to action. This tactic is very useful especially at the end of a text. The call-to-action encourages the user to click on an ad or interact with the brand. Users will know what to do to get the information they need and will be guided by your words in this discovery process

What persuasive copywriting is

Often, those who write online content do so to encourage readers to take an action (call-to-action). For example, to subscribe to the newsletter, leave a contact, purchase a product or service and much more. To do this, there are specific rules that take the name of persuasive copywriting.

Persuasive copywriting starts with an analysis of the characteristics of the product, even compared to competitors, and uses the right words to convince the public of the goodness of its choice.

Persuasive copywriting takes into account the needs of users, those who drive our every action. The text must be specific, describing and recounting every detail: the more exhaustive it is, the more you have the chance to convince the reader.

People need to be able to touch the product through

words, just as if they were seeing it in front of their very own eyes. Persuasive writing, in fact, touches the emotions.

Most of the time people buy on impulse, following the flow of their emotions. A good copywriter knows how to strike the right chords to be able to hit this goal. For this it is necessary to know the rules of persuasive co-pywriting.

To arouse emotions, a good copywriter tells rather than describes. When you write to convince someone to buy something or to take an action, it is a good rule to turn the text to a positive form. Eliminate "no" and "not" from sentences, this is a simple trick that will give you many satisfactions.

People read the beginning and the end, but what is in the middle is usually skipped. Readers are distracted and on the internet are in a hurry so they pay attention to the opening sentences, then they quickly scroll th-rough the text and read the conclusion. In light of this data, the most relevant information in the text should be inserted precisely in these sections.

Without a call to action there is no persuasive copywriting. It is unlikely that someone will perform a certain action on their own initiative. People are naturally lazy and you have to guide them through the purchase. A good call-to-action is direct, short and gives an urgent character to the reader.

A final important role in persuasive writing is that of testimonials. In fact, the positive feedback of people who have already purchased a product or service are very important, especially on the internet where things cannot be seen and cannot be touched. Word of mouth remains one of the best advertisements ever, and consumers tend to trust the reviews of other consumers more than they trust you as a business.

The last rule for persuasive copywriting is to always remember that a good text puts the people who read it at the center and from here it starts to develop the different concepts. Who are the readers? It is necessary to speak their language correctly if you want to capture their attention.

Examples of good copywriting

Copywriting, therefore, allows us to have creative and

persuasive texts, which accompany different types of publications: from the blog post to the advertisement, from the tweet to the product sheet for an eCommerce, examples of copywriting are everywhere.

To better understand what we mean, we have selected three particularly successful examples, which apply copywriting to different types of text.

1. UrbanDaddy

UrbanDaddy frequently sends emails to its customers, recording high open rates, thanks to a secret ingredient. Every email UrbanDaddy sends is fun, right from the subject of the email.

The company avoids long preambles to the message, so readers don't feel like they're wasting time reading that email. The tone of voice is a mixture of the classic promotional slogan and irony, to emphasize the fun aspect of the product.
The company knows its audience and knows it can joke to grab attention.

2. Trello

If you are into social media marketing, you certainly know Trello, a very useful tool for team project management and daily task management. But perhaps you've never stopped to consider the copywriting aspect of its site.

The product description is clear and written in a very simple style. All features are listed in a single sentence that reassures the user.

The images are also integrated with an explanatory copy that allows you to immediately understand all the features and methods of use of the tool.

3. VISA

Despite being one of the most used credit cards in the world, Visa has identified an emotional distance between the brand and customers.

So the company decided to create the GoInSix campaign: a series of interactive content to motivate people to eat, shop or travel, using six-second videos, six-image cartoons or just six words.

The campaign worked on all social channels, also thanks to a particularly successful copy, based on a very familiar formula for customers: the to-do list, re-thought in an emotional key.

We advise you to dig deeper into these 3 case studies as they will show you how important it can be to have a good copy.

Chapter 19

SEO Copywriting

Now that you have understood the importance of copywriting for your ads, it is time to discover what a good copy can do for your business in terms of ranking your site on Google, the most used search engine in the world. This is where SEO copywriting comes into play.

The definition is pretty simple.

If copywriting is the art of writing persuasive and conversion-oriented content, SEO copywriting is the art of combining this content with search engine optimization.

How can we not consider today the enormous possibilities offered by the Internet for every company? Impossible. And what is the best way to be found by potential customers on Google? Of course, writing relevant content - interesting and useful, capable of responding to user searches - and optimized for SEO.

A copywriter today cannot ignore the correct use of metadata and the consistent publication of content to aim for the best indexing on different search engines.

Knowing the structure of an online article, knowing how to correctly use h1, h2, meta description and keywords is essential when copywriting for the web.

Good and informative content now accounts for about 50-60% of what allows you to reach the best search engine rankings and if having good writing skills is already a skill, being able to implement SEO-optimized writing is a true double benefit.

Below you can find a list of the essential features to keep in mind to produce content from a SEO perspective.

- Use the h1 tag for the title and the h2, h3 tags, and so on for the paragraph and subparagraph titles. This helps Google to identify that your article has a well defined structure, allowing your article to rank higher.

- Use keywords in a natural way in the text and use its variants (singular and plural, synonyms, antonyms). Repetition is not seen very well by search engines, so be creative.

- Use bold, italic and underlined consistently. A well formatted article is what Google wants to ses.

- Use meta tags. These help a proper formatting of the article, keep them in mind.

- Use bulleted and numbered lists. For some reasons, Google loves lists. Try to insert them in every article or long-form post you publish.

- Rename the files and images using the keywords in the title, fill in the alternative text field.

- Use internal links and external links that are useful, consistent and relevant. Cross-references are what build the internet. It is important to insert links in every content you publish, no matter the platform, as this will give users a broader experience of your brand.

- Insert links on relevant anchor text. Of course, links have to be put in the right place. Do not paste them at the end of an article, rather hyperlink them at a proper place.

Chapter 20

Copywriting as a Career

Like we have done in a previous chapter, in this book we want to give concrete career opportunities as well. We understand that not everyone is meant to be an entrepreneur and social media marketing offers many pathways to those that are willing to take up the challenge. Becoming a copywriter is definitely a suitable option for many. Here is more information about this.

You may have thought at the beginning of this chapter that being a copywriter is a job that anyone can do: "You just need to know how to write in English!" you might have said to yourself. But we are sure that by continuing to read you will have realized how many skills and knowledge are needed.

The way to become a judge, notary or teacher is always very clear: a degree, a few years of internship, a state exam or a qualification and if you pass all this, you are in. Obviously we are simplifying the concept here, but only to explain that to become a copywriter often the path is not so linear and defined. There are endless ways to create a professionalism that goes beyond knowing how to write well, even if the basics are the same for everyone.

First of all, you have to focus on your training. A bachelor's degree in humanities or at least some training in this field will certainly make your life easier, but you can't think that you are already a professional copywriter after publishing a few dozen articles on a blog.

Even without taking writing courses, you can start from the material you find on the internet to understand how to write quality content. Sign up on LinkedIn and Facebook groups on the subject to find opinions, suggestions and insights, and then read, read a lot, read anything, especially advertising related material.

Another useful suggestion is to start specializing immediately on a few topics, to be deepened and studied in depth, based on what your passions are, but always following lines related to the business, for which there may be companies interested in having you as a producer of their content.

Having your own blog is not essential, but it is certainly a great exercise, especially to train consistency in writing. You won't always write about what you like or when you like. Being a job you will need to be able to develop those techniques that allow you to really do it for work.

Use Google Analytics and the Google Search Console, accompanied by other SEO tools, to refine this aspect in your articles.

During the training phase, also accept some free collaboration if the one who proposes it to you can offer you a benefit in exchange, such as a training course or simply the opportunity to mention the collaboration that is so important in your CV.

Take courses, including online ones, to specialize on specific topics and acquire new skills in Digital Marketing, SEO strategies and Social Media Marketing. You will have many more arrows in your bow than the competition by learning from the best professionals in the sector.

Becoming a copywriter depends a lot on your ability to experiment and look for different paths for your training, but you should also have some basic skills. These are the following.

- Know in depth the language in which you will write the texts: a grammatical error from a copywriter is unacceptable;

- You must like writing: don't think of becoming a copywriter just to work from home or because you imagine it to be an easy job;

- Have creativity: the copywriter is not a writer, but his ability to use the word must be close to that of an artist and the same is true for his ability to use figures of speech and turns of phrase;

- Know how to adapt: as in all freelance jobs, customers will always be different and it will be up to you to reconcile their requests with your professionalism, proposing the right tone of voice and thinking about the correct target;

- Never stop studying: even writing like the web and social media is constantly evolving and even current events can affect your texts, so, once again, read, read a lot and stay updated;

- Be patient: as we said, not all customers are the same and not everyone will always do well with your work. The important thing is to understand the goals and try to achieve them together. Varying the work until it is perfect.

Job opportunities for copywriters

Hiring a copywriter is an excellent idea for any type of business, from startups to large companies to small and medium-sized businesses.

In fact, everyone deserves quality content.

"Content is King" has become a kind of mantra in recent years, and for this reason the copywriter is becoming one of the most sought after positions in the new economy based on social interactions.

The ingredients to earn a place of preference in the arms of recruiters will naturally be transversal skills, able to range from the choice and creation of the visual aspect of the communication, to the SEO optimization of the content produced. No improvisation, then, because if even the best happen to make mistakes, precision for a copywriter will have to be one of the main directions during job interviews.

In short, for companies, hiring a copywriter is becoming increasingly essential, regardless of their size, because knowing how to say the right things in the right way gives seriousness and professionalism to the brand and offers new opportunities for contact with potential customers.

There is no shortage of job offers. Just do a simple Google search to check how many ads it is possible to find throughout your state, you will be amazed.

Depending on the experience and skills acquired, a copywriter can earn up to 5.000 dollars per month. Everything, as usual, however, depends on the companies you work with, on the projects you are committed to and on your level of professionalism.

Freelance or company copywriter?

There are several options for copywriters and aspiring copywriters: from freelance work, excellent especially at the beginning for the classic apprenticeship, to working in a company as an internal resource.

Today more and more companies are able to seize the huge opportunities of digital marketing and social media marketing and for this reason having a copywriter in the company means having a person dedicated to the production of all company texts. From copy for social channels to texts for informative materials, print, up to the content for the corporate blog, you name it: everything that requires some sort of writing is done by the copywriter.

However, the freelance solution remains the most flexible one, as a freelancer is able to guarantee autonomous organization of working times and methods, as long as it has a solid personal organizational base.

Chapter 21

Instagram for Social Media Marketing

The second social media platform we are going to discuss is Instagram.

On Instagram, companies have the opportunity to meet a community of over 1 billion active users per month and more than 500 million active users every day.

Instagram offers you the opportunity to convince your audience to take a certain action through the creation of visual content, hence visual marketing and recently a new vertical video format that is changing the consumption of content. We are referring to Instagram

TV.

Wondering how you can improve your Instagram presence and create an active community around your brand? Here's how to take advantage of all the opportunities.

Instagram users love to connect with your brand

According to Iconosquare, as early as 2015, 62% of Instagram users followed a brand on this platform. Instead, according to a Forrester study, Instagram was found to be offering businesses 58 times more opportunities for success than Facebook and 120 times those of Twitter.

Forrester looked at the top seven social networks, six of which showed that companies manage to achieve a user engagement rate of less than 0.1%. For Instagram, this value reaches 4.21%.

The incredible level of interaction that can be achieved is given by the faithful and active nature of Instagram users.

Building your brand or educating your customers is a central part of any successful business and Instagram plays an extremely important role in this regard.

Instagram's rapid rise continues, detracting from Snapchat and Facebook's stagnant growth rates. This large audience is now a strong draw for IGTV the video hub just launched by Instagram. While IGTV's monetization possibilities are already foreseen in the future, content creators could gain new exposure and build their fan base even stronger.

It is proven that social networks have an increasing influence on users' purchasing decisions, after all that is what social media marketing and this book are all about.

By finding the right mix of relevant content you will have the ability to attract more interest in your brand and push your users without having to invest too much in presentations and expensive marketing activities. In fact, the numbers we just showed you clearly paint a picture where Instagram is the go-to channel for brands and companies that do not have a big budget to spend on social media marketing, as the attention on Instagram is currently undervalued.

Why is Instagram a unique social network? Here are the main reasons.

- It is fully mobile
- It is based on visual design
- It has practically no links

To be successful on Instagram it is not enough to post beautiful images and photos randomly. On the contrary, it is necessary to follow these rules.

- Have a clear vision on goals and strategy
- Publish with a constant frequency
- Be familiar with your followers
- Have a well-defined style guide

By combining all these ingredients, you have the opportunity to reach your audience directly and in a focused way, to increase their interest, increase brand awareness and see impressive results in terms of return on investment.

The first fundamental step in an Instagram marketing strategy is to define the goals you want to achieve. You can apply the SMART method we discussed in chapter 7.

Even if you have never used this platform or you are starting to use it and the results have not arrived yet, it is important that you have specific goals in mind to achieve.

In this way the contents produced can be focused on reaching them and will be more consistent in the eyes of your followers and customers.

Companies usually use Instagram to showcase their product or service, build a community, increase brand awareness, tell the story of the company and its values, increase brand loyalty and share news and updates.

It is very important to choose one or two goals to pursue. We advise you to choose 1 to 2 goals from this list.

- Promote products or services
- Building new relationships

- Show behind the scenes of the company
- Introduce company personnel
- Representing the most informal and fun part of the business

The creative opportunities and visual aspects of Instagram - if you strategically use Stories to show the personality and faces behind your brand - can be especially powerful for highly visual businesses and a great way to creatively engage customers and employees, reach out to your potential customers and build relationships with them.

Once the goals and metrics for evaluating achievable results have been defined, it becomes important to understand which audience you want to target.

The main focus of marketing is to communicate the right message to your audience just when they want to hear it and knowing the demographic characteristics of the user who uses a platform is a central element to understand if you are reaching the target audience or not.

This is why we recommend that you start by immediately defining your buyer persona, as described in previous chapters. We hope you are starting to see how everything is connected together in social media marketing.

Once you have defined the goals and determined the effectiveness of Instagram for your target, you can get to the heart of your strategy following some simple steps.

1. Optimize your profile
2. Create an editorial plan
3. Define the timeline of your posts
4. Measure the returns on your effort

How to optimize your Instagram profile
When someone searches for a keyword on Instagram such as "lighting design", the list of accounts that will be displayed are those that have the keyword in their profile name.

The order or ranking of these accounts will depend on how Instagram determines that they may be of interest to the user researching that term.

If someone you follow follows an account associated with the keyword you enter, Instagram will show you that account and include this information in the list. This immediately gives the user a reason to choose yourself from everyone and build more trust.

Think of your Instagram profile as a homepage.

In your profile you have the possibility to share some information about your company and to insert links to send traffic to your website. So, the real question becomes how you can optimize your Instagram profile.

By making the most of the four elements below you will be able to create high value for your users:

The company biography and description
The description must be closely linked to the brand. What you choose to share in the short space made available by Instagram must be representative of your story, your offer and your values and must be able to explain to users what you do. In addition to this, companies tend to insert a slogan or a tagline as in the case of Nike's "Just Do It". Larger companies can also

choose to include their hashtag within the description.

The profile picture

It is very important that your brand is immediately recognizable when a user looks at your post or visits your profile. For most businesses this means using their own logo, a brand (the logo minus some words) or a mascot as their profile picture.

The links

Unlike other social networks, Instagram doesn't allow you to add links to posts. The only part where you can add links is in your profile's personal information. Many companies tend to use this link to bring users to their homepage, however it is also possible to use this possibility to drive traffic to a particular landing page or content. Only available to verified Instagram account holders, there is the option to add links to Instagram Stories as long as you have reached 10,000 followers or more.

Instagram Business Profile

In July, Instagram released the news of the launch of a new tool that is very useful for all companies: the Business Profile.

Currently, this feature is still being tested and is only available in the United States, New Zealand and Australia, but will also be available in other countries in the coming months. With this new tool, companies will have the opportunity to link their Instagram profile to their Facebook page, have insights and statistics on followers and posts and promote targeted posts to achieve pre-established goals directly from their app. In this way you will be able to know which posts are more successful, on which days and in which time slot your target is most active and who your audience is on Instagram. The news does not end there. With this new feature, in fact, users will have the ability to get in touch with the company with a simple touch on the "Contact" button directly from the app.

Optimize your Instagram feed for business

To be successful on Instagram you can't overlook any element so you have to pay attention to how your profile looks as a whole.

Your feed is the first opportunity you have to make a

good impression and entice people to hit the "follow" button. And since your Instagram profile is becoming as important as the homepage on your website, you need to make sure it lives up to it.

When someone visits your Instagram profile, they'll decide in seconds whether or not to follow your business by quickly scrolling through your feed, reading your bio, or clicking on the highlights of your stories.

When it comes to converting visitors to followers, it's no longer just the photo editing style that needs to be consistent.

Fortunately, it's easy to create a professional-looking feed with a well-curated and cohesive Instagram aesthetic.

Gorgeous Instagram aesthetic isn't a new trend on Instagram. Companies of all sizes, from startups to super brands, have been curating their feeds to attract new followers for a very long time now.

Your feed doesn't have to adhere to the all-white, with

perfect Instagram minimal aesthetic images to be successful, it just needs to be consistent with your brand and target market.

What's important in 2021 is that you make sure every aspect of your feed and every post aligns with the aesthetic you've chosen for your brand.
So whether you're posting to Instagram Stories, posting an IGTV video, or creating profile page highlights, you need to make sure everything lines up and represents your global brand and Instagram aesthetic.

You can plan the look of your Instagram feed and aesthetics using a third-party Instagram marketing platform. Today you have many options available in this regard, just do a quick research online.

Use a good photo editing program or app
When it comes to editing and enhancing your photographs, a reliable photo retouching program with features that can speed up operational time is what you need.

This is a good investment in not only making your Instagram feed good-looking, but also getting more Instagram followers.

Creating a cohesive Instagram feed can be achieved by using the same 1-2 filters or presets on each photo.

This greatly simplifies the merging of all your photos and also reduces editing time.

Chapter 22

Content Strategy for Instagram

Photo and video content are the heart of Instagram. The more than 100 million photos and videos shared every day on the platform are proof of this.

But what should the content you post be about?

Before thinking about the visual content, style and design it is useful to define an overview of the message you want to convey and the topics you want to cover. Some companies focus on their product (as does Nike Running, for example), others on community needs and their culture (as WeWork does).

Content is King but Context is Queen, remember that.

In terms of content strategy, on Instagram as for any social network, there is no precise rule to follow. It all depends on the context in which you operate but above all on your buyer persona, or rather, what you might expect to see and interact with your ideal customer.
The important thing is to create content that is able to interest and engage your followers and that allows you to achieve your goals.

For this reason, the starting point must be to build the fundamentals on which to then develop the contents.

All companies, regardless of size, sector or geographic location, have the ability to share quality content on Instagram. This content can relate to the stories of the people who make up the company, the corporate culture, the product and its uses, demonstrations and so on.

The contents most shared by companies are the following.

- Behind the scenes
- User generated content (through re-sharing)
- Product demonstrations and showcases
- Educational contents (guides)
- Cultural contents able to show the ethics and values of the brand
- Fun and entertainment
- Customer stories and case studies
- Team presentation

Before deciding on what type of content to focus on, it may be useful to brainstorm to collect ideas and then formulate the content marketing strategy.

Tell a story

The future of Instagram marketing is all about telling a story with your photos.

As with all content, the quality level continues to rise in social media and brands that want to break through, especially on Instagram, will have to prioritize the great over the simply good, even if it means reducing the frequency of publication.

On Instagram, it helps a lot even if your feed tells the same overall story through notable content and iterations. If your content ranges in many directions, it's very difficult to gain devotees who share a common infatuation with a specific topic.

Instagram is inundated with mediocre messages from brands who forget that the social network is supposed to be a "visual inspiration platform".

Fascinating audiences through images, videos and stories, don't just advertise. This is one of the secrets to having success on Instagram.

Instead, become a storyteller, offer "micro-stories" through captions, videos, Instagram stories and Instagram profiles and thus increase engagement rates.

Authenticity is a winner

In 2020, Instagram did a lot to cleanse the platform of bots, fake likes, fake "influencers", and make malicious services that sell fake followers cease to exist.

Furthermore, Instagram continues to fight not only against automation apps, but also against users who take advantage of them. If you resort to artificial tools that automate your online presence you may see some of your Instagram features removed as a form of "punishment" for using bad practices.

Edelman's 2020 Trust Barometer found that 60% of people no longer trust social media companies. Being able to be perceived as trustworthy is fundamental, so make sure you do everything you can in this regard.

Create authentic content, tell stories with your subtitles and use Instagram Stories features such as emoji, slider, gif or question sticker to increase engagement.

Because of Instagram's algorithm, creating beautiful and engaging content isn't enough to increase your engagement rate.

You need to set up daily routines that will help you get more engagement. Like, comment and interact with your audience or potential followers, don't just go social, be social.

It is vital to commit for at least 10-30 minutes before and after the post is published, plan the posts but also comment, share and create Instagram stories on it.

Here are 3 success stories that showcase the importance of doing what we have just told you.

- The pillars of the Saturday Night Live Instagram profile are behind the scenes of the show and exclusive clips reserved for followers.

- FedEx's Instagram profile focuses on visual content regarding the means used by the company to make its deliveries such as vans, trucks and planes. Their feed is a mix of artistic and exciting photo content.

- Oreo, on the other hand, puts its product at the center through fun and highly engaging content. Often they insert funny phrases within the images and use very colorful and consistent backgrounds to make their posts stand out within the platform.

6 Fundamental Steps for an Effective Instagram Content Plan

Once the themes have been defined (which, however, can always be revised based on the results of the campaigns) it is time to bring them together into an editorial plan.

This way you should be able to define the style and design of your posts and how often you post content.

To have a coherent profile on Instagram and be able to convey the right message, it is important to follow a precise style that reflects that of the other marketing channels used. In this regard it is possible to create real style guides to follow when creating content. These are the points to keep in consideration when doing this process.

- **The composition**. It refers to the positioning of elements within the visual content and, more generally, to the structure of the photo or video. Not all marketers are expert photographers, so it may be useful to define some rules regarding the background, the main focus of the content and the space needed for text at the top or bottom of the image.

- **Color palette**. Always using the same range of colors you have the possibility to create a consistent and focused feed. Warning! Defining a series of shades to use doesn't mean depriving yourself of the possibility of using other colors, but it will help you give a familiar touch to your content. A good idea is to choose a color range in line with the one usually used by the brand in other marketing channels, in this way users will more easily recognize your company and, consequently, your brand. We have extensively discussed this topic in a previous chapter, feel free to get back to it for reference.

- **Font**. If you insert quotes or texts within the images you post on Instagram it is important that you are able to create coherence also through the fonts used that must be in line with the rest of the corporate communication.

- **Filters**. These tools can turn even the photos taken by the most inexperienced photographers into a high quality picture. Filters can drastically change the look of your photos and videos, so it is important to choose to use only some of them (those most in line with your message) in order not to confuse the user. Using a different filter for each post creates confusion and disorientation in your followers who will no longer easily recognize your posts.

- **Caption**. Instagram provides more than adequate space for image descriptions, once this limit is exceeded, the text will be truncated. This space allows you to further differentiate your content and take it to the next level. There are various ways to use this space. Some use it for micro-blogging, others use it to insert a catchy short title or to ask users questions. The possibilities are endless. The important thing is to always make sure to maintain a certain consistency in what you do.

- **Hashtags**. They have become the most used tool on social networks to categorize the content produced and posted. On Instagram, hashtags allow users to discover new content and accounts to follow. If you want to avoid putting too many hashtags in the caption, a good method is to include them in the comments. By analyzing the hashtags most used by your users before choosing the ones that best suit your content, you can ensure that you reach a wider audience.

Hashtags are extremely important. Like emojis, they are much, much more than a fad used by teenagers. They provide a mechanism for users to quickly navigate through topics of interest by grouping posted messages with hyperlinks.

Choosing the best hashtags for your Instagram posts can make a big difference. Make your hashtags too generic - think #christmas or #fashion - and your post will face competition from millions of other competitors. Instead, use a mix of industry-specific trends and hashtags to find the best topic to connect with your targeted followers.

The number of hashtags you use is also crucial. Even though Instagram allows up to a maximum of 30 hashtags per post, a mass of hashtags under the caption risks appearing untargeted and unprofessional. That's why 91% of top brand posts use seven or fewer hashtags to get lots of likes and comments.

What is the right frequency to post on Instagram?

There is a lot to be said about the consistency and frequency of publications on social networks.

The consistency and frequency with which you post content can help your audience understand when to expect new content from your company, and keeping a constant schedule allows you to maximize engagement without taking breaks or lengthening the silence times when they do not see new updates from you.

A Union Metrics study shows that most brands post on Instagram daily with an average of 1.5 posts per day but this number should definitely not be taken as an indicator.

This study also shows that there is no correlation between an increase in posting frequency and a decrease in engagement as companies posting more than two content per day saw no negative returns.

How nice is it to have a community just waiting to hear the next thing you have to say? This is what creates a planned and relevant editorial plan.

Develop content by creating a pipeline of automated messages that are released based on a defined schedule

As if it were a subscription service, this aspect of an effective Instagram strategy becomes fundamental. Routine meets users' expectations and builds trust by fueling their needs.
To generate constant growth, our advice is to post at least two or three contents a day and experiment with an additional post to understand which type of message best suits your reality and the needs of your audience.

To determine the best time to publish, use a service like Iconosquare or the excellent Co-Schedule. Both these tools work pretty well and we cannot recommend them enough.

These powerful tools provide detailed analysis on a wide variety of aspects, including optimization.

When is it the right time to post?

With the recent changes in the algorithm that manages the Instagram feed, timing is one of the elements taken into consideration by the platform to decide what content to show to users. This is why it is important to post in the time intervals in which your target is most present on Instagram to get more engagement.

According to a research conducted by CoSchedule, the best days to increase engagement on Instagram are Mondays and Thursdays between 8am and 9am (EST).

Obviously, this data comes from a wide-ranging research so it may not reflect the habits of your target. For this it is very important to find out the Instagram habits of your followers using the Statistics function of your Instagram account. This helps you identify when your followers are most active and allows you to plan accordingly, making sure your posts continue to appear at the top of their feed.

Even if you see most of your followers being active on Instagram at a specific time (usually in the morning and in the evening after work), that doesn't mean your posts will perform better during that time. This is due to the increased competition in those time periods which make it harder to reach the top of the feed on your followers accounts.

There's more engagement on Instagram on weekends (22.3%), so it might be worth scheduling some posts for Saturday or Sunday.

Posting during the weekend with the planning offered by third-party solutions is easy, but you need to find time to respond to messages and comments even on Saturdays and Sundays. If you have a personal brand, you should be accustomed to this anyways.

Once the themes, the frequency of publication and the times for posting have been determined, it is useful to draw up an editorial plan in which to report all the content to be posted and the relative timing.

Unfortunately, Instagram does not currently allow you to program posts directly within the platform itself. However, in order to do so additional software such as UNUM, Planoly, OnlyPult, Later, Instapult and TakeOff can be used.

Interact with your followers and drive interactions

You can simply post your own images, but we've found that success comes when you're proactive in the community you are trying to create.

Invite your followers to interact with your content.

A good way to drive engagement is by using interactive content. Interactive content engages your audience more, increases click-throughs, and offers more opportunities to educate and delight your network.

Create any type of action that stimulates user involvement in your content, in order to activate the algorithm that consequently will allow the content itself to reach as many people as possible.

For this purpose, you can use open or closed questions, ask people to answer a survey, or ask yourself about Instagram Stories.

Imagine each of your posts as an opportunity to interact with your followers. Give your fans something to do and watch how the interactions increase like wildfire.

Obviously don't misrepresent this advice, not every post should contain a call to action. Diversification is key in this regard.

It becomes essential instead to understand that you do not have to ask to buy your product every time, give their email or share your page with everyone they know. It is much more subtle what you are asking.

You need to ask your followers for something that makes them feel good about doing it or reaffirm their values or goals. With this method you can get even 300% higher interaction than a simple publication.

Each post is an opportunity to create interactions, increase conversions and interact with your community. Publishing your content must force users to do more than just "digest" a photo. For explosive growth, users need to push themselves to share your content. Every element of your Instagram post should offer the ability to drive interactions and build your network.

Interactive content helps you increase your engagement rate

According to Forrester, Instagram engagement, measured by consumer likes, shares, and comments is 10 times higher than facebook, 54 times higher than pinterest, and 84 times higher than twitter. Do not sleep on this amazing opportunity and integrate Instagram in your social media marketing strategy.

How to measure the results of your Instagram marketing strategy

Tracking your performance and results is essential for any social media marketing strategy you want to implement.

Doing this allows you to understand which content is most interesting to your audience and allows you to optimize your strategy to take steps toward your goal.

By paying the right attention to the growth in the number of followers, likes and comments on your posts you have the opportunity to understand what is actually working (and therefore bringing results) and what needs to be improved.

Measuring the engagement rate on Instagram is very simple: add the number of likes and comments to your post and divide it by the number of followers you had at the time you posted.

If you want to make more accurate measurements, you can choose to use ad hoc measurement software, social media management or social CRM tools capable of tracking performance, monitoring trends, monitoring the use of hashtags, measuring user engagement and managing multiple profiles.
In this regard, the sentiment analysis tools that allow you to detect when users are talking about you and their attitude towards your brand become very useful.

Chapter 23

Increase Engagement on Instagram

In this chapter we are taking a look at six practical and quick tips to implement for the growth and increase of engagement on Instagram. If you have gone through the other chapters, you should have no doubts about the importance of having an active community.

1. **Leverage the content posted by your users**

   Instagram users provide your business with a large number of quality content. Curating the content posted by your users helps you create an active and interactive community and incentivize your audience to share creative content that shows their way of interacting with your product or service and their relationship with your brand.

2. **Leverage the content posted by your employees**

   Employee-generated content receives eight times more engagement than company-shared content. Additionally, employee content increases brand awareness by more than 500%. Your business needs to get employees involved in content creation right away. Companies with engaged employees are known to outperform their competitors; engaging employees in content creation can help create a sense of common purpose.

3. **Include people in your posts to increase interaction**

   Georgia Tech analyzed more than a million photos on Instagram and found that photos showing real people get 38% more likes and 32% more comments.

4. **GIFs are better than photos**

   GIF format is more eye-catching than photo. GIFs are shared more than JPEG or PNG formats, and are more expensive and more effective than producing video. GIFs inspired Instagram to create boomerangs that record a short sequence of still images before combining and scrolling them back and forth, ready to be uploaded to the platform. The tool has already produced excellent results for brands that have pioneered this futuristic means of increasing Instagram engagement.

5. **Convert Instagram Followers to Email Subscribers**

   Email remains the conduit for building truly deep customer relationships. This is why brands strive to convert Instagram followers into email subscribers. First, create a clickable bribe in your Instagram posts depending on your target audience. For example, consider offering a reward, free content, or a discount. Once the audience clicks, make sure your landing page includes a strong call to action linked to an email submission form. Finally, create an email list to effectively engage your new email subscribers so you can start developing more meaningful relationships with them.

6. **Share your Instagram posts on Facebook**

A Buzzsumo study of over 1 billion posts on Facebook, shared by around 3 million company pages, highlighted how content shared directly from Instagram gets more engagement than those posted directly on Facebook. Promote as much as possible your Instagram channel.

For example, promote your Instagram account on Facebook by making a Facebook ad with a clickable link to your Instagram page. You can also take advantage of Instagram's auto-post and cross-promotional tools. Cross-promotion tools allow you to instantly post from Instagram to Facebook, Twitter, Tumblr, and more, bringing followers together across your social networks. Remember not to cross-promote all your Instagram posts on other social channels or you risk "cannibalizing" your content, negating the

need for followers to visit your Instagram channel in the first place.

Chapter 24

Instagram Direct and the Rise of the Dark Social

Since 2018 there has been an increase in the use of Instagram Direct which, with the addition of GIFs, videos and lately also audio notes, has transformed from a simple one-to-one vehicle to a solid group chat platform. To date, it appears that people are not only actually using this feature, but that it is even becoming a popular alternative to Messenger and WhatsApp.

Thanks to its features, on Instagram Direct it is always easier to start a private conversation and share or copy and paste links with someone on Instagram. Of course, that includes interacting with businesses as well.

So if you don't have a DM strategy in place, it's time to think about it. DMs can be great for customer support, branding humanization, Instagram audience research, increasing sales and conversions, and so much more.

This phenomenon is called Dark Social. Here is the definition of it.

Dark Social refers to all those communications between the company and the target audience (or between the users themselves) that cannot be measured in terms of likes, shares and comments.

However, using a "dark" customer care you have the opportunity to better understand the sentiment of your audience, as well as to have a direct measure of the level of loyalty of your followers.

You may think that the dark approach is suitable only for small and medium size businesses. Well, in reality, even big corporations can get quality data from the "OTC" interactions they have with their customers.

Chapter 25

12 Advanced Tactics to Increase your Sales on Instagram

Doing Instagram marketing isn't that simple. Soft skills and knowledge of some tools are required to get started. But the rapid growth of Instagram is also accompanied by an incredible increase in interactions from users.

In fact, some studies have shown that brands on average get 25% more engagement on Instagram than other social networks. Impressive right?

It means that Instagram is a great place to increase brand awareness but also drive sales. The real million dollar question is: where can you find marketing tactics that really work on Instagram? In this chapter we have collected 12 of the most effective strategies you can apply to turn your company Instagram page into a money making machine.

Tactic #1 - Use advanced influencer marketing

Until a year ago not everyone knew the meaning of the term influencer. Today it has forcefully entered the common language. Social marketers who have had satisfactory approaches with influencers in the past, are now faced with very different scenarios.

Influencer marketing has acquired multiple aspects and has truly become an indispensable component of your marketing strategy.

If you read further you will discover the very advantageous opportunities offered by what we could define as the most humanized and authentic marketing strategy of the moment with the necessary exceptions and clarifications.

Consider that there are more than 60,000 influencers on Instagram covering all vertical markets including fashion, beauty, health and wellness, home decor, nutrition and more.

In order to keep their followers and their branded offerings, expect "authenticity" for 2021, as we have mentioned in the chapter dedicated to this year's trends. The days of overly edited posts and photos and comments with Instagram bots are over, leaving room for more authentic experiences and relationships.

Aligning your brand with influencers who truly love your product and are excited to share with their followers is an ideal way to build an authentic relationship on Instagram, as well as get better engagement and outcome.

Adding Instagram influencer marketing into your overall Instagram strategy can help you increase your brand awareness, grow your follower base, and generate more sales.

Instagram influencer marketing has become increasingly significant these days, allowing marketers to collaborate with leaders, industry experts and push brand messaging to a wider audience.

According to a Nielsen report, 92% of consumers trust the recommendations of individuals (even if they don't know them) more than brands. Using trustworthy, reputable and nice people is a great strategy to use to market your brand.

The future of Instagram marketing will increasingly be about relationships and influencer engagement. Since influencers are considered "independent" personalities, aligning your brand with their authoritative voice can add authenticity to your message.

Algorithms continue to favor people over brands and the challenges of creating authentic and engaging visual content for users, given the competition, make using influencers your assurance to continue being heard on Instagram.

However, selecting the right influencer can be difficult.

Plan an influence strategy that includes a short trial period to see how receptive the network of followers of the influencer specifically selected for your brand is. You also need to make sure that your influencer is provided with the tools, resources and guidance needed to effectively perform their role, that they work side by side with you on the campaign as a true partner.

New collaboration strategies increase social media impact

2020 saw an interesting trend on Instagram that has begun to redefine how brands collaborate with influencers.

While before, most brands sent products to influencers and expected to see a sponsored post in their feeds and stories, now brands are considering taking influencers on vacation.

The premise is simple. Choose the most influential Instagram influencers with millions of followers, send them to hang out in a luxury hotel, let them try the products, and of course let them post all about them.

In this way, fashion brands like Revolve or Boohoo took small groups of Instagram's most followed influencers on vacation, and benefited from their followers in successful campaigns.

The strategy is to curate and coordinate perfect content, in postcard places for perfect images, but also rough shots that showed the brand from other angles.

The tactic is to prepare an exciting adventure, with Instagrammable meals and other offline experiences, allowing influencers to show how the product or service fits into a perfect lifestyle that influencer followers obviously aspire to. Obviously, you should not neglect to include links for purchase in the content of the influencers.

These types of operations, if well prepared, cost a lot.

The ads created, however, are not short 30-second TV commercials, but a series of posts and stories that leave a much longer impact for the brand. Plus, you can promote your brand hashtag, harness the power of user generated content, and reuse the shots for a campaign.

Collaborate with more authentic influencers and therefore more prodigal also towards the

brand

"Authenticity" is another great Instagram marketing "trend" in 2021.

Are the days of Instagram posts with perfect poses, overly edited photos and comments on Instagram bots over, leaving room for authentic experiences and relationships?

2020 saw the rise of a new generation of authenticity-focused Instagram influencers, such as Jenna Kutcher, who garnered over half a million followers in one year, going from 166 to 700k + without ever paying for a single follower.

The influencer marketing industry has exploded thanks to Instagram and global advertising spend for influencers is projected to reach $ 5-10 billion by 2021.

While brands are excited about influencer marketing, regular Instagram users are starting to see beyond perfect, sponsored Instagram posts.
In order to maintain their followers and their partner-

ships with brands, Instagram influencers are expected to become more personal and authentic in 2020. This includes conversing about sponsored content, with influencers coming to thank their followers for supporting their sponsored posts, and explaining how much of their income comes from their business.

The influencers of 2021 build their success by giving continuous evidence of their greater transparency and authenticity on Instagram, they show that they really consume the products of their sponsoring brands, buy them and repurchase them, even going so far as to exhibit the empty packaging. This simple gesture can represent the new genre of influencers, more trustworthy and authentic, more valuable to brands.

Brands are also beginning to give indications in the sense of authenticity

One of the best ways to create authentic brand partnerships is to think long term. Start thinking about the influencers you work with as brand ambassadors and create longer one-year contracts that include multiple interventions per month.

Aligning your brand with influencers who truly love your product and are excited to share with their followers is an ideal way to build an authentic relationship on Instagram.

Having influencer posts consistent with your brand for an extended period of time not only increases brand appeal, but helps their followers start matching your brand with that influencer, which can lead to better engagement and results.

Micro and nano influencers for the best engagement rates

Bigger isn't always better when it comes to Instagram marketing, a reality that many famous influencers face now as brands start working with micro-influencers (accounts that have fewer than 100,000 followers).

"Nano-influencers" are also on the rise, as brands choose to work with average users, with a 1000 follower base, on sponsored posts and brand campaigns.

Nano-influencers are a secret weapon of social media marketers. Nano-influencers have a following of around 5,000 followers but work in a very specific niche. They represent the typical geek friend, which is appreciated on social media.

Although their following is much smaller than that of a celebrity, their community is more involved with what they post.

Two separate studies by HelloSociety and Markerly found that influencers with a smaller following have a much higher engagement rate than top-tier influencers, and both studies noted a drop in engagement rate as the size of the business audience.
According to a Digiday survey, nano-influencers are able to engage up to 8.7% of their followers, while the engagement rate of famous influencers, who have more than one million followers, is only 1. 7%.

Partnering with influencers from smaller accounts is not only cheaper, it can also be more effective.

These types of marketing campaigns with nano-influencer and micro-influencer marketing are set to take off in 2021 as brands take advantage of authenticity and algorithms more.

But in 2021, it's not just influencers who benefit from a smaller and highly engaged audience - micro-brands or micro-brands are also on the rise.

Micro-brands are no different from a small company, there is nothing "small" about them.

Micro-brands on Instagram compete with large retailers and are able to generate millions of dollars in revenue with small teams thanks to the power of their data-driven design and low cost of customer acquisition using social media.

Thanks to the hyper-targeting capabilities of Instagram ads, micro brands are able to design and sell products created for a very specific customer, which they can then target on Instagram. Big brands are starting to take notice of their smaller competitors and respond by creating their own in-house micro brands.

These examples are also helpful in demonstrating that people crave more personalized and targeted content, and this year they will quickly click the "don't follow" button if they aren't resonating with the content on your feed.

If you want to keep Instagram followers in 2021, create targeted content for your ideal customer. Use your Instagram analytics to see which content is resonating the most and that your Instagram follower demographics match those of your customers.

Tactic #2 - Leverage on Instagram to position your brand to the maximum with storytelling

The best way to position a brand is to tell a story that people want to hear, right? And what better way to tell a story using visual content? Our brains are "wired" to understand 60,000 images faster than text. This means it is easier for people to understand the message when using images in your strategy.

Here's where Instagram comes in handy. As you probably know, Instagram is 100% visual, every brand needs a story that differentiates their products from other brands, and Instagram is the best social network for sharing visual content.

By posting images that support any type of storytelling that relates to your brand, you can have a better positioning in your audience's mind.

Tactic #3 - Use hashtags wisely to increase engagement

Twitter may have invented social media hashtags, but Instagram really knew how to exploit them and now creating a hashtag strategy on Instagram offers many results.

Selecting the best hashtags for your Instagram posts can mean the difference between appearing as a top post or sinking to the bottom of the feed without a trace.

Nowadays, Instagram hashtags not only rank content and make it searchable by users, but are an effective way to gain more followers, increase engagement, and broaden brand reach and awareness.

Make your hashtags too generic and your post will face competition from potentially millions of others. Instead, use a mix of industry-specific trends and hashtags to find the best hashtag to connect with your targeted followers.

If you want to harness the potential of the platform to reach huge audiences, increasing the role of hashtags on your Instagram is the way to go.

According to research by Agorapulse, Instagram posts with at least one hashtag got 70% more likes and 392% more comments than those without hashtags.

With the decline in organic reach and the rise in paid impressions, with algorithms being introduced to get brands to pay for exposure, hashtags still represent the best way to organically drive your social marketing campaigns, leveraging on social media posts.

Dig deeper into the hashtag research
Researching hashtags before using them is important, as the more relevant and targeted the hashtags are, the more you increase the chances of reaching a target audience who will interact with your published content. Use Instagram hashtags in a targeted manner

There are many studies on how many hashtags to use in each post to increase engagement. Depending on which study you rely on, the best number of hashtags is between five and the maximum allowed number of 30.

An analysis by TrackMaven found that using 11 hashtags in each post is optimal for increasing engagement on Instagram.

The reality is that the key to Instagram hashtag success is to use them strategically, regardless of whether you decide on three deeply researched or 30 carefully chosen hashtags. You have to be as specific as possible with the hashtags it also limits the targeted user pool, which makes it easier to build a highly engaged audience.

Add hashtags to your Instagram profile bio for conversations and shares

Since the Instagram bio only allows for a standard hyperlink, adding hashtags encourages people to start conversations and share experiences around your brand.

Instagram hashtags can now be inserted into profiles, a feature that provides an extra boost by providing a link to the hashtag feed, however, don't expect to make your bio detectable in the hashtag search results.

Enter "#" before each word in your profile and it will automatically become a clickable link that can be used for anything like promoting the Instagram community you are creating.

Use special daily hashtags to engage and inspire your content

Daily hashtags offer a way to engage with your audience every day, keeping them constantly engaged with your content and connecting with them over the long haul.

Use a balanced combination of general, niche, and location-based hashtags.

Include a brand hashtag in every Instagram post. Use a hashtag for the campaign.

Insert hashtags in Instagram Stories to attract new audiences

Adding hashtags to Instagram Stories - in text, a sticker or a location tag - gives your content another way to be found by new audiences.

But inserting hashtags in images or videos of Instagram stories does not guarantee to reach large slices of new audiences because it all depends on the quality of the content published and their level of engagement.

Organize or join a live event, whether it's a conference, event or vacation, this is the time when people are most engaging in seeing what's happening in real time on Instagram. So making your story visible to others is a great way to get new eyes on your Instagram profile and get more followers.

When your story is added to the location story, you usually get a notification from Instagram. When a photo or video of your story is visible on a hashtag or location page, you will see the name of that page when you look at who has seen your story.

If you go to your Instagram explorer page, you will see the live story for the current city you are in, but your story only has the option to be inserted if you add a location sticker to your Instagram Stories.

Tactic #4 - Cross promotion to grow your followers faster

Most users and brands don't, but cross-promotion (or just co-marketing) is one of the most effective ways to grow your following on any social network.

You can ask one of your stakeholders to tell their followers about you and to follow you, so you can do the same thing with them.

The problem is that initially this practice had become practically spam but now the situation has certainly changed and when co-marketing of this type is carried out with elegance, it can be truly effective.

The biggest mistake when it comes to cross-promotion is sending requests to the wrong people. In order not to waste time, it is very effective to exchange a few messages before starting a real launch, making sure you are natural with a direct and clear message.

We cannot forget Instagram Pods

In recent years, the fashion of Instagram Pods has exploded, also known as Instagram Engagement Pods, i.e. groups (public or private) in which users try to trick the Instagram algorithm to get more followers, likes, comments and views.

The goal of these groups is to increase the engagement of their Instagram profile from real and active users by exchanging likes on posts, and possibly leaving a comment.

There are several ways to access Instagram Pods. Some being public do not need specific rules, others being private, however, require an invitation from one of the members of the group.

The benefits are certainly immediate. The increase in engagement is quick, just take the time to "like" everyone on the pod, hoping they will return the favor.

The disadvantages?

Obviously this practice is not without its pitfalls. First

of all, the engagement rate could be staggered, and it could even decrease rapidly if it is not practiced continuously.

So consider all the pros and cons that this would entail and then decide if Instagram Pods groups are right for you to grow on Instagram. Generally speaking, we find this to be a bad idea for everyone that is serious about building a community of potential customers.

Tactic #5 - Use Bridge Marketing to increase sales

Have you ever heard of "Bridge Marketing"? It's when you build a bridge between your business and a specific niche so that more people can feel drawn to your products or services.

For example, let's say that you are starting a company in the sector of industrial lighting and you are looking for specialized designers with whom to start a partnership.

While this type of user is browsing, he may come

across an "ad" on Instagram promoting the following message.

"We specialize in industrial lighting, find out more here".

This is nothing more than making sure you segment Instagram Advertising campaigns and create personalized ads for each segment.

As with Facebook, the more specific the segments you are going to create (thanks to the segmentation based on Gender, Place, Age, Niche) and the more useful messages to your audience you can take advantage of.

Tactic #6 - Use videos to communicate the message behind your brand
Most brands have now adopted video marketing, and the frequency of video posts on Instagram has gradually increased over the past few years.

Video marketing on Instagram is the opportunity for a company to show the world who they are and what they do in a minute or less.

People want connections, relationship personalization has pushed to come face to face with your followers, whether it's Instagram stories, Instagram tv or a good old video post.

One of the principle of the moment is: explore the full range of Instagram video formats.

A picture may be worth a thousand words, but a video is worth millions. There is no comparison with the effectiveness and popularity of online video content.

Instagram recognizes this and offers a suite of video options that greatly entice marketers.

For example, consider Instagram Stories "live video" option to reveal new products or services or use a pre-recorded ad to deliver authentic behind-the-scenes stories to your followers to communicate the brand and increase engagement on Instagram.

Less refined videos work best on Instagram Stories

For a long time, brands have been posting very sophisticated videos on Instagram to attract customers. These videos require time and financial commitment to be produced and with the Instagram algorithm it is not possible to grasp the results of the dawn of the platform.

Today, however, less refined but genuine videos, which cost less time to create and publish, work best on Instagram. Instagram users, for the most part, are not interested in watching highly polished videos, preferences have changed over time, but they are looking for content that is authentic and relevant to them.

Invite your employees and managers to talk freely on video about their challenges, in order to promote your company culture. This tactic works incredibly well to increase engagement.

Tactic #7 - Use analytics tools to identify content that generates the most interaction
One of the biggest mistakes people make when managing social media is posting content they "think" will be of interest. Yes, sometimes you can get a fluke and

people react very positively to the content, but most of the time this doesn't work.

It is much more effective to share photos or videos that have a proven record of success.

Tactic #8 - Start on Instagram and finish on Facebook

If there are still few people promoting certain products or services on Instagram, it means that there are still huge opportunities available.

An example? Iconic, an Australian fashion and footwear eCommerce, after launching an Instagram campaign to raise awareness of their brand among Australian women and boost sales of new collections, launched a Facebook campaign that targeted the same interests the following week.

The results? Women who viewed the campaign on both Instagram and Facebook converted 23% more than other active campaigns.

Instagram campaigns have increased brand awareness and increased purchase intent while direct ads to the

Facebook website prompted people to complete the purchase.

In summary? Launching visually compelling campaigns on Instagram to increase brand awareness, then continuing the campaign via direct ads to increase sales via Facebook is a great way to get the most out of your advertising efforts.

As you can see, Instagram can be an extremely interesting tool that can generate sales when you know how to use it correctly.

Tactic #9 - Guide users through the conversion funnel

For most brands, getting a large number of followers is important but turns out to be just one step in the funnel of global marketing activities.

To move users further down the conversion funnel, any way to capture your followers' email should be considered. And one of the best ways to capture these emails is to ask for it in exchange for something.

Share an image with a call to action and insert a link in the caption on how to download an eBook or subscribe to your newsletter.

Once the user is engaged in this way, it will be possible to proceed step by step to a complete conversion, continuing in another way (through marketing automation actions or one-to-one relationship marketing actions).

To do this, however, it is necessary to create a targeted and tailored landing page. From there it will then be possible to push users through your different channels and keep them updated with your products or services.

Tactic # 10- Mix videos and photos
One of the hottest trends in Instagram marketing is to mix photos and videos in your strategy.

Considering that a video can generate three times more shares than posts made of images only, video is a valuable tool that can be used to engage followers and grow your following and thus the traffic to your website.

For example, take a look at Oreo or McDonald's on Instagram and you'll see impressive examples of stop motion videos using a product to generate ironic and often incredible storytelling.

Videos can be fun, shareable and engaging, and with Instagram's video editing features, great results can be achieved with ease.

In stop motion, for example, simply hold down the Record button and pause when you want to shoot a different scene. Or you can simply upload a pre-recorded video.

Tactic #11 - Host contests on Instagram

Contests are a powerful engagement tool on Instagram, generating 3.5x more engagement and 64x more comments than regular posts.

Despite this, they are regularly neglected by brands: only 2% of them organize contests. This means there is a huge, relatively untapped resource for marketers to leverage.

Organizing a contest on Instagram obviously requires planning a strategy, defining goals and rules and creating posts that attract attention.

The most frequent are the "Repost" contests where, in case of victory, the prize consists precisely in the repost of the winning profile on the social media and other web channels of the promoter of the competition, in this case leveraging people's visibility and ego. Or you can also opt for contests that offer cash prizes or similar: we have already talked about weekends in luxury hotels or shopping vouchers and they make up for a great prize for a contest.

Tactic #12 - Shopping on Instagram

If you run an e-commerce business, you cannot fail to take advantage of one of the new features available on Instagram: the shopping function. This feature allows you to insert tags in your posts and this for followers means to "tap" on the image to see all the information useful for purchasing a product such as the price, the name of the article and the link that refers to the e-commerce page.

The new feature like Shopping in Stories this year has helped advertisers place the shopping bag icon on whatever product or service they are promoting.

With this option, marketers have the ability to target their audience to click on the shopping bag icon and view the product image, information and website link to purchase the product. With over 400 million users using Instagram Stories on a daily basis, advertisers can take advantage of this marketing feature to connect with their target customers.

The idea that users can go from inspiration to action with the click of a button and buy directly without leaving the Instagram app is a winning opportunity for brands, for Instagram, and for shoppers. Please, make sure to include this tool in your social media marketing strategy, as it is a very important one.
For now, only about 20% of marketers actively use shoppable posts, with a vast majority admitting they haven't yet noticed an increase in sales from shoppable tags.

However, shoppability remains an Instagram trending

goal, as over 50% of Instagram marketers plan to use more shoppable posts in 2021.

The future of marketing is on Instagram since many Instagram users follow popular brands on this platform (around 80% of users follow at least one brand on Instagram)

Instagram seems to have taken up the challenge of becoming one of the cornerstones of the online shopping experience, with brands and retailers that can use the shopping features to allow followers to purchase items directly on the platform.

There are many elements that can lead you to this important strategic conclusion.

Instagram is focusing more and more on brands also with the introduction of more in-depth data analysis, useful for companies to regulate their activities in the adoption of purchasing functions on the platform.

Shopify, which has more than 500,000 merchants, is helping online retailers expand their offerings on Instagram's shopping features.

Since 2019, Instagram allows you to buy not only from

feed posts and stories, but also from explorer posts and videos. Also, Instagram allows you to have your own "Shopping" collection for easy browsing.

Instagram shopping features will be an important part of the platform in 2021. So find the easiest way for your brand to leverage direct-to-consumer sales as part of your overall Instagram marketing strategy.

With Instagram out of the way, we now have one more social media to focus on in this book. We are talking about Youtube and the next chapters will tell you everything you need to know about it.

Chapter 26

Youtube for Social Media Marketing

ouTube needs no introduction. However, we want to emphasize that it is the place where billions of people place their eyes every day. The interesting fact is also that these eyes do not belong only to a particular category of people, but to every demographic.

You will certainly guess what this can mean for your company's marketing. But how do you effectively use this channel to promote and grow your business? Let's browse a bit among the channels of this Social Network and see what we can understand.

YouTube is teeming with bizarre, often frivolous and

sometimes even nonsensical (at least in appearance) videos uploaded mostly by teenagers or young adults. So before writing this book we asked ourself how your business can apply a serious marketing strategy in this context.

If one of your buyer personas coincides with these millennials (about 18-24 years old), some hypotheses could even shyly peep out. And, in any case, in such a crowded channel your videos would have to outperform some very tough competition to get to be seen by your target audience.

Do not worry, there is a way to use Youtube in your social media marketing strategy. In fact, there are many strategies you can apply and in the next few pages we will try to give you a blueprint you can follow to engage with your target audience using Youtube.

Let's start on our journey along the 7 YouTube Marketing tips we have put together for you. Destination: your success.

1. Publish videos, not advertisements

You will soon find that traditional forms of advertising don't work on YouTube. You will need to experiment with other ways to advertise your e-commerce, website or business.

Even company presentation videos or product demos don't give great results unless they're particularly creative.

When creating video content to upload to your company's channel, take the time to think about why and how your audience should like and share it. The shareability factor is in fact as important as the idea behind it and the quality of its implementation.

YouTube is a community made up of real people who want to give in, feel and interact with other real people. The link with your company or your brand is greatly strengthened if the public can associate a face with it, preferably the one most representative of the entire organization.

This move can profoundly change the dynamics of interaction, which go from watching a video of a company to building a relationship with a human being. Aiming for interpersonal relationships therefore becomes a long-term strategy that can make your company acquire customers for life.

The face of the company must obviously appear as much as possible in the videos but also in the header of your channel and in the previews of the contents. Another winning strategic move is to include sections of personal life within your business, if you can do it without feeling like you are forcing it. Allow your audience to have a sneak peek behind the scenes, see your project take shape or find out how you started this career. This transparency adds depth and color to your marketing.

2. Publish videos on a regular basis

Many users who start using YouTube for their company's marketing strategy open a channel, upload a couple of videos to it and soon get discouraged because they don't reach the desired goals in terms of subscriptions and views. From the initial enthusiasm they then move on to abandoning the company, with a fair amount of frustration.

Gathering an audience around your YouTube channel is a process that takes time and patience. Focus on creating valuable content in the best possible quality. Promote your channel: announce it on your blog, on your mailing lists and on other social platforms on which you are present.

As you do everything in your power to promote your channel and videos, remember to engage with the followers you've already gathered. Take care of these people who, in a boundless sea of possibilities, have chosen to follow you. This means replying to any comment as soon as possible and, if some of your followers have a channel, visit and comment on them as well.

3. Youtube is not the end

For most businesses, a YouTube marketing strategy can't stop at attracting subscribers and views. Of course, this is the first of the goals, but once this is achieved there must be a further step towards converting these users into customers. To do this you will probably need to create a bridge between YouTube and your site.

Include a link to your site in the first line of each description you write for your videos.

Insert a link to the About us section of your site in the header of your channel as well, as this will allow you to cross promote your content on different platforms.

Study methods to ensure that is the user itself that moves on your site. For example a video in two parts of which the first is available on YouTube and the second only on one of your company web pages is a great tactic that you can use to reach this goal.

4. Build partnerships with other content creators in your sector

Another very effective tactic to power your YouTube efforts is to partner with an established creator. This can happen in different ways and forms, but for most companies it will probably involve the investment of a certain budget to offer to one of the YouTubers best suited to your goals.

Take some time to select the right people to collaborate with, as this is fundamental. Choose them from those who have at least 100,000 subscribers and who exert a significant influence on your target audience. Once you have identified your influencer, you can make him different proposals. You can ask him to create a video according to your requests, appear in your video, talk about you or your products in one of his productions.

These characters are generally very protective of their community and the role they play in it. They are therefore understandably very selective in evaluating the collaboration opportunities they receive: offer them something they can genuinely feel in their hearts and you will be more likely to receive positive feedback.

5. Put a lot of focus in creating engaging thumbnails for your videos

YouTube is the second largest search engine after Google - of which it has been a brother since 2006 - and the two get along very well. Even if the Google algorithm is almost top-secret, it seems that a YouTube video with the appropriate meta data compiled properly has more ease of acquiring a high ranking than an equally optimized blog post.

Not only can your videos therefore appear in Google search results, but they also do so with a thumbnail that provides a visual preview of the content. We talked about the great effectiveness of images in our recent article on Social Marketing in a previous chapter, but you can definitely confirm the phenomenon in the normal everyday experience you have when browsing Youtube.

6. Do not forget about keywords

Check out the Google Adwords keyword planner to see which keywords are the most popular within your target audience. Next, use them to create content relevant to these topics and include them in the titles, tags and descriptions of your videos.

7. Do not forget the call to action

This is an essential point when it comes to using YouTube for professional reasons. If it is possible you need to insert a call-to-action at the beginning and at the end of your videos. After all, you want your users to take a certain action, once they appreciate your content, right?

The content is in fact a tool to capture attention, perhaps entertain, inform and create a relationship. At some point, however, this attention should flow into something that also benefits your company moneywise. This could be simply filling out a form, sharing the video with their contacts or visiting a specific page of your e-commerce.

The possibilities are endless, and the effectiveness of your choice will also depend on the creativity you will be able to employ in grasping them. Check out YouTube's policies, make sure your idea doesn't conflict with any of the points, and then let your creativity run free.

Using YouTube for your business could become a vital part of your social media marketing strategy. Nothing, in the current data, suggests that there is a halt in the growth of online video on the horizon. On the contrary, the more you wait to focus on that part of your target audience, the more your business will risk falling behind your competitors.

Chapter 27

Youtube Ads

Creating a YouTube video campaign with Google Ads is a great way to improve your brand awareness. Today, video is the most popular format consumed by users. Why do people love videos? Because it can be a source of information, as well as entertainment. It is easy to consume and contains graphical and visual elements that are much more appreciated than a written text.

That's why taking advantage of Youtube advertising can be a decisive element for your marketing campaign. To create a Youtube ad is not necessary to be a professional videomaker, many times even DIY ads can lead to many conversions and positive results. The important thing is to set up the campaign in the best way possible for your goal.

This chapter is going to tell you more about it.

How do you create a Youtube ad?
The platform that allows this operation is Google Ads. In reality, Google Ads includes different types of campaigns, such as search and display campaigns. In this chapter, however, we will focus only on the video aspect to understand how to use them in a successful social media marketing campaign.

Advantages of video campaigns on Youtube
Why create video campaigns on Youtube? Because basically this solution leads to numerous advantages. A marketing campaign on Youtube can be set up and configured in different ways, depending on the specific target you want to reach. Here are the main advantages:

Video is better than written words
Due to the digital revolutions of the last decade, the feeling that reading is much more challenging than consuming audiovisual content has crystallized in the

mind of your target audience. The so-called "Storytelling", so dear to bloggers, is now increasingly moving towards the video format. Videos have the strength to entertain and not tire and often generate great curiosity in viewers, which is fundamental for an effective marketing campaign.

Greater engagement

Videos have a much higher engagement rate than written texts. So, creating Google Ads campaigns on Youtube is the best solution to reach users in today's advertising reality.

High visibility

Youtube is rated as the second most used social network in the world. Recent research has established that on average a person spends 40 minutes a day watching videos on Youtube. A video campaign on this channel is therefore one of the best options for gaining visibility from users and for lead generation.

Flexible offer

One of the characteristics of advertising on Youtube is the enormous flexibility you have as a company and as a user. For example, most commercials can be skipped after 5 seconds. In this case, Youtube does not charge the advertiser, which is a pretty neat feature if you ask us.

Reduced costs

Youtube is cheap. This is a great thing, although it probably isn't going to last for very long. The cost for advertisers is reduced mainly for two reasons: there is not much competition and at the same time the number of videos and content posted on the social network is very high. This results in a very low cost per campaign ratio and therefore makes it very appealing for every social media marketing campaign.

Measurability

Youtube, like all social platforms, allows you to analyze insights, or understand how your ad is doing. For example, you can see how many people have watched your ad, how many ignored the ad, the demographics of those who saw the ad and many other useful information for developing data driven marketing campaigns.

Choice of the relevant target audience

Even with Youtube campaigns it is possible to choose precisely the target audience, allocating the invested funds only to those who fall within your own market niche. The evaluation can be done using different parameters: interests, personal data, behavior and much more. Again, you can see how important it is to have a buyer persona in mind before starting any form of online advertising.

Distinctive element

The fact that Youtube is still little used as a channel to create advertising campaigns means that it can become a distinctive element compared to the competition. Using a video format when everyone chooses written words can be the winning card of your social media marketing strategy.

The most effective video campaigns

There are several options for creating a quality video campaign. In particular, the most efficient video ad opportunities are four. Let's see them in detail.

TrueView in-stream

These are advertising campaigns that can be displayed before, during or after a video. They are very interesting because it is also possible to activate them in Youtube videos that are linked in other sites.

These campaigns are minimally invasive for users who are not interested, as they can be skipped after only 5 seconds of viewing. This feature proves decisive for advertisers. For those who want to reach many users, the first 5 seconds become essential, so it is advisable to develop visual content with modern and captivating graphics, capable of catching the user's attention in a few moments.

Out-stream

This advertising format differs from the in-stream in that it is created specifically for mobile and tablet. The out-stream format is designed to facilitate interaction with the hand in spite of the mouse.

How does it work? Out-stream advertisements are hosted by Youtube partner sites and appear in a social news feed or while we scroll through the site text. Their appearance is closely linked to the scrolling of the page and requires manual action to be viewed or skipped.

TrueView video discovery

To sponsor videos on Youtube, an excellent alternative can also be the TrueView video discovery option. These are the ads that appear in Youtube search results, both on the home screen and in the side column that appears when you are viewing a video.

Why could video discovery ads be beneficial to your company marketing campaign? First of all, their strength is the CPV bidding strategy, which is different from the traditional Pay Per Click, or the ability to pay only when there is an actual view. Secondly, it is important to underline the fact that these ads can also be viewed from mobile, which, compared to other techniques, helps to increase the visibility of your message.

Bumper ads

Bumper ads are the new frontier of video advertising. They cannot last more than 6 seconds and appear suddenly while watching content. Usually these are advertisements with very little text, often high-emotional content and the immediate presentation of the product or service.

Their main characteristic is speed, as users are not able to skip them. They are heavily exploited in the mobile environment, because on devices users skip in-stream ads much more frequently.

Their cost policy is also very favorable: one charge every 1000 views.

Optimize your Youtube ads

How to best optimize a video campaign on Youtube? To obtain satisfactory results it is good to follow some useful tips and to implement adequate strategies. Here is a powerful list of tips you can implement from the start to improve your results.

1. **Diversify campaigns.** It is better to create a large campaign with many goals or many small campaigns each with its own goal? Without doubt the second hypothesis. Diversifying allows you to optimize your budget and allocate it more carefully to the most important campai-

gns. At the same time, creating separate campaigns allows you to analyze the results more precisely and evaluate the information of the users who interacted with them more extensively.

2. **Create an attractive Call to Action.** "Edit the call to action", this is the name of the Google Ads button that allows you to insert a CTA that can ask the user to perform a certain action. It is important that the call to action is interesting and pushes the viewer to watch the video in full or click on a link.

3. **Choose the best video category to show your ads on.** When you set up a Google Ads campaign on Youtube you can choose which video categories to show it on. It is necessary to set a specific video or a video category. It may also happen that the ads are applied to a non-performing video, where the content is not targeted properly. For this reason, it is a good idea to constantly monitor the results of your campaigns so that you can make the necessary

changes to maximize their results.

4. **Analyze data**. Without data it is impossible to determine whether a video campaign on Youtube is generating the desired results or not. To have an optimal response, it is good to analyze the numbers and parameters throughout the campaign. Among the indicators to consider there are the CTR and the percentage of views. The CTR (Click-Through rate) indicates the number of people who click on the ad, taking as a basis the total number of people who see the ad. The views percentage, on the other hand, analyzes the relationship between people who saw the ad and the number of impressions; this analysis is essential to understand how many people have skipped the ad and how many have watched it in full.

Mastering video campaigns on Youtube with Google Ads can be an excellent solution for brands looking for visibility and exposure to their target audience. It is an advertising technique that is not yet widely used and in which there is less competition than in other channels. Our advice is to keep it in consideration when you are creating your social media marketing strategy, as it can be an effective way to interact with your target audience.

Chapter 28

The Importance of a Company Blog

Having a corporate blog is an essential requirement for all businesses today. Please, don't commit the mistake to think that, since we have talked about social media platforms up to this point, we do not recommend having a company website. This could not be farther from the truth.

Those who decide to open and manage a corporate blog do so to promote their products and services to their target audience. But creating and managing a corporate blog isn't easy.

We imagine that you have realized this as well, if you

have tried to do social media marketing before reading this book.

Probably many times you have thought about creating a blog for your company or personal brand, but you did not know where to start, or the people you turned to did not achieve the desired results. Who knows how many times you have thought that your articles do not receive visits, that users do not read your content and you have never found an answer to the reason behind this lack of results.

The management of a corporate blog is in fact a complex and very extensive activity that requires an investment in terms of both time and money.
For this reason, we would like to tell you that it must be entrusted to expert people who know how to promote specific marketing campaigns. Working in this direction means investing a lot in your business and creating corporate value for the various stakeholders. We suggest you take this approach even if you are working by yourself.

A corporate blog is neither an encyclopedia nor a box

to be filled with intrusive advertising. The strategy behind a blog is to create and disseminate interesting content to your target audience. Period, end of the story.

However, putting this into practice is difficult and requires commitment and a creative effort.

What we are saying is that to open a blog you need to have a strategic plan designed ad hoc. In this chapter we are going to show you the right approach to have when considering the idea of having a blog for your company or personal brand.

Outline your business blog goals

First of all, to aspire to have a successful blog you have to understand what your goals are when you are creating it.

For this reason you will have to ask yourself specific questions:

- Why should we start a blog?

- What do we want to communicate with my blog?
- What are my ultimate goals for this blog?

Having the answers to these kinds of questions clear will allow you to start off on the right foot. Please, set the goals for your blog using the SMART method.

The importance of contents of a corporate blog
When you start writing on your business blog the first question you need to ask yourself is the following. What kind of content do we want to post?

It must be something that is easy to understand for the user, which allows him to immediately put into practice what he has read, which offers a solution or comments on an issue that is important to him and which has a link with the products and services offered by yours. company.

Each blog page must deal with a particular topic and theme related to your business, it must not contain news from other sectors or personal information since it is not a personal diary.

Publish the right amount of articles per month

You have to schedule your content, make it interesting and publish it with a certain regularity and frequency.

You can't think of having a corporate blog if you publish a post every now and then.

Try not to spend months between the publication of one post and another, but write constantly and follow a pattern. You will have to try to publish at least one post a week, especially in the first period, and you will have to make sure that those who read you expect to find your content published on that precise day, for example every Monday, Tuesday, etc.

This way you will create a routine and a fixture for readers who will be enticed to return willingly to your blog.

Choose the writer

Not everyone is good at writing, as we have seen in the chapter dedicated to copywriting.

Entrusting this task to a person who does not have the appropriate skills could be a really big mistake.

If you do not have professionals in the sector within your staff, contact the agencies that develop corporate blogs. They can create a tailor-made content marketing strategy for you. In the immense ocean of the web, there are many corporate blogs and the competition is high.

The blog is like a goldfish swimming in the ocean depths and must be found (by users) in the midst of sharks and other ferocious fish species that inhabit the seabed.

We used this metaphor to tell you that to bring more and more readers to your corporate blog, you need to worry about promoting it as well.

To gain visibility online, developing an SEO strategy is essential.

In this way, in fact, your content will be able to rank high on search engines and be easily searchable by users. Furthermore, you should allocate a part of your budget to paid advertising to always intercept new users interested in your content.

The advantages of a business blog

Whether you run a small business or a large company operating in any sector (agriculture, industry or service), you are likely wondering if having a blog is really worth the time and effort.

The answer is definitely yes. Blogging is a relatively simple and inexpensive way to improve your marketing strategies, drive visitor traffic, and attract more customers.

Statistics from Hubspot's Inbound Marketing Report highlight how important it is to have one. In fact, according to the study, 57% of companies that have a blog reported acquiring at least one or two new customers a day.

Furthermore, about 81% of companies say that their blog is useful for supporting business activity and interacting better with consumers.

A business blog helps you make money

Creating a corporate blog is a good starting point for earning and obtaining a return on investment and, for this, it is necessary to take care of the blog on a daily basis and draw up an editorial plan before starting to post.

Although at first it can generate a monetary spend, in the medium to long term the investment will bear the desired results and will generate an excellent return on invested capital.

This is why it is important to create a blog that allows your business to take off from a reputational point of view, but above all in terms of ROI and sales volume.

Improve the SEO positioning of your blog
Search engines favor corporate websites that publish content that is updated, valuable, informative and of great added value. If you pay attention to SEO optimization, the search engines will reward you.

An important fact is the following. Blogs offer on average 434% more indexed pages and 97% more indexed links.

Remember that when you publish a blog post, SEO optimization is essential to appear high on search engines.

Increase the reputation of your company

Writing "fresh" content that is rich in advice and information helps to accomplish the following goals.

- Increase the visibility of your brand;

- Contribute to the improvement of your reputation and the good positioning of your company within the sector in which it operates;

- Outperform the competition;

- Become a leader in the industry in which you operate;

- Build loyalty with your audience;

- Build brand awareness.

In fact, every quality article is a way to communicate to customers and visitors their competence with respect to the topic and the reference sector.

You can link it to your social channels

Sharing topics and articles from the blog to social networks (Facebook, Twitter and LinkedIn) helps to increase customer engagement, brand loyalty and, consequently, monetary income.

Give a "human face" to your company

Creating a corporate blog allows you to create a "virtual" space where you can show users and customers your true spirit and philosophy of your company.

By sharing your experiences, case studies, presenting new products and evaluating industry news, customers can take a look at what is the essence of your business.

In essence, the blog gives your business a voice.

Differentiate yourself from the competition

A corporate blog helps you differentiate yourself from the competition, forces you to think about the latest trends, industry news, your customers and the world as a whole.

Blogging also helps you outperform the competition

and position your company as a leader in their sector rather than a follower.

You get to know your customers

Through a blog, you have the opportunity to obtain interesting key information about your audience and actual and potential customers, by monitoring the topics that receive the most shares and comments.

You can do quality link building

The positioning of your blog on the search engine also depends on incoming links. Thanks to well-written posts and content, you can attract high quality reposts from other websites, which will allow your blog to rank even higher. It is a virtuous cycle and we suggest you take advantage of it.

Remember that quality content is important because it gives you value and with it you can improve your ranking on Google.

How to create a corporate blog that outperforms the competition

Corporate blogs are certainly an innovative and much

more effective advertising tool for one's business than ordinary and more traditional ones.

It used to be possible to advertise your business simply with an ad or a banner, but today the consumer wants more. He wants to identify with the company, he wants to know its history and also to receive useful information from it for his daily life.
The corporate blog therefore not only has an advertising function, but also serves to give the consumer exactly what he is looking for, which is a great story.

That is why it will be vital to follow some guidelines if you want to build a successful business blog. Here are few points to keep in mind.

Focus on a story
To be successful with your business blog, avoid using it as a simple advertising tool.

Instead, the blog must become a connecting channel between the company and your potential customer, or rather a collector of stories. Try to use it, therefore, to spread important news about your business, to tell something about you and your company.

Mind the style of writing

A corporate blog cannot be built without taking into consideration important elements such as the writing style and even the graphics. Writing in correct English is the basis, avoiding mistakes and excessive repetition is a must.

Try to capture the customer's attention with graphic elements that are captivating. From titles and bold, to the presence of real images and other multimedia content.

Give your customers a voice

A great way to tell a story on your business blog is to give your customers a voice.

In particular, ask them if you can tell and share their past experiences or if they themselves want to write a few lines about you.

Of course, always be honest: don't make up anything, but emphasize the positive aspects of the story you're going to tell in your post.

Observe your competitors and learn from them

You are not alone in your market, so being able to understand what your competition is doing can be a great way to improve your corporate blog even more from both a marketing and brand awareness point of view.

Study what others are publishing so you can be inspired

You don't have to blatantly copy the blogs of other companies or other professionals, but you must always try to be original with respect to them.

Analyze the results of your blog to keep improving

After writing the contents of your corporate blog, you need to understand if they have achieved the desired results.

To analyze the performance of your blog, use tools that are also made available by Google, such as Google Analytics.

You will be able to know how many visits you have received, how users interacted with you and so on. In this way, your company blog will not remain a tool for its own sake, but you will also be able to understand if there are any sections to improve.

To give you an example, there may be articles that do not bring traffic to the blog and therefore will need to be updated or even taken down, as they penalize the overall SEO score of the website. Monitoring the results of your blog is the only way to improve it in the long run.

Chapter 29

6 Rules for your Company Blog

We always observe these 6 rules to create a corporate blog that is effective and that reaches the goals it was created for.

Here are the six rules for creating your business blog.

1. If your blog is not on the home page of your site, you should place a button or link in the navigation bar that directs users to the blog. If you don't have a navigation bar, you need to create it.

2. This button must contain the phrase "Blog". You could also call it "Read the blog", or "This is the blog." You do you, try to stand out from the crowd. The important thing is that people easily identify it as a blog.

3. If your blog does not have infinite scroll (like Tumblr for example), that is, if the reader cannot continue scrolling down indefinitely, at the end of each page you must insert a button that connects the reader to the following pages. "Next Posts" or "Other Posts" are good options for the name of this button.

4. At the end of each post, enter a sharing space or section containing related articles. In short, your reader should not be disoriented once they have read the entire content of the article. This solution is useful for decreasing the bounce rate and keeping viewers on your site.

5. If you offer a particular service, you should give the reader the opportunity to subscribe to that particular service. It could be the RSS feed of

your blog, or a newsletter, or even a "Follow me on Twitter or Facebook" option.

6. If in the last 3 months you have used your blog to post links to your podcast or your videos, don't lie to your audience, call this space differently and no longer a blog. And above all, try to correct this and create a useful blog to improve your brand and generate more traffic to the site.

7. Finally, remember to interact with users who read your blog, so as to improve the general User Experience.

Now that we have discussed these simple rules, it is time to dive deeper into the actual strategy to market your company or personal brand through your blog.

Chapter 30

Winning Strategies for Generating Leads through a Company Blog

We have discussed how a blog is a corporate communication tool that fits within the inbound marketing strategies of a company. Having a corporate blog is not enough, you have to optimize it to reach more customers and potential clients.

This means, you need to create a powerful lead generation strategy that not only gives visibility to your company, but that attracts qualified users to convert into customers.

What are the strategies to implement to generate leads through a company blog?

To generate leads you need to implement 5 winning strategies.

Before talking about these, we want to clarify immediately that Lead Generation is defined as follows.

Lead generation is a set of marketing actions aimed at acquiring a contact list of site visitors who are really interested in the activities carried out by a company.

It is not merely a question of increasing the traffic and popularity of your blog and business site, but it is about stimulating blog visitors to make a purchase on the web and to increase sales.

Think, for example, of a doctor's office website. In addition to making the blog attractive with content and informative guides that are interesting for the public, the goal is to transform contacts into real customers who make an appointment with the doctor and benefit from the performance and services provided by the clinic.

Through this business model, it is the site visitors themselves who express their interest in the products and services offered and get in touch with the firm, the company or any other professional who has a company website or blog.

You can ask your visitors to just leave their data in an online form to be contacted or to obtain specific communications in exchange or to receive free advice.

Now let's dive deeper into the different strategies.

Strategy 1 - Content Marketing
Writing words is not enough.

The web is full of content, articles, posts, but most of them have little use and little value for users.

A valid Content Marketing strategy begins with plan-

ning and developing useful content that has informative power and is of great added value for the audience.

What editorial content do you need to develop?

Posts, articles, guides, infographics, webinars, interviews, research, videos, tutorials are the main tools
that act as a lead magnet or a "magnet" able to attract
the interest of the public to visit the company blog and
conclude a purchase of a company product or service.

A very useful method is to give users the opportunity
to read the blog in exchange for some benefits, such as
being able to receive exclusive offers and discounts,
perhaps even inviting users to subscribe to your newsletter.

Always include calls to action at the end of your posts.
Invite your readers to do something at the end of each
article, this will increase the engagement and the overall conversion rate of your social media marketing
strategy.

Thanks to this little tactic you have the possibility to

create a blog to convert leads into real customers.

Strategy 2 - Use Social Media

Interacting and communicating with social media has become increasingly strategic for every company and every professional, don't you agree? We bet you do if you have read this book up to this point.

How important is it, for example, to communicate and make yourself known on Facebook?

On Mark Zuckerberg's popular platform you can select the market segments to target thanks to the Facebook campaigns service to generate leads. Thanks to this service, you have the ability to "target" posts and content based on the audience you want to reach.

It is an economical and fast strategy that ensures concrete and fast results: the Facebook ad form is very easy and intuitive to fill out.

Strategy 3 - Email Marketing

How important is sending emails to the potential audience you want to reach?
A lot.

Once your business blog has started generating leads, you can use the email addresses obtained to turn them into active customers.

Email marketing is a winning strategy that guarantees a good economic return on investment: recent research has shown that about 66% of consumers have made an online purchase following an email marketing message.

Furthermore, users and visitors of a corporate blog who receive personalized offers and promotions via email spend 140% more than those who do not. To turn your mailing list into a powerful lead generation machine, you need to make sure your emails are relevant to your blog's prospect profile.

Strategy 4 - Landing Page

Why are businesses using a landing page more and more? That is a good question.

The answer is simple. They do it to collect the email addresses of visitors to the corporate blog so that they can be transformed into leads. To get a potential customer's email, it is important to offer free resources such as e-books, reports, guides, checklists, etc.

This will encourage them to subscribe to the mailing list: use few fields in the forms, otherwise users may desist from leaving their contacts.

Strategy 5 - Dedicated events
To build loyalty and to generate leads to be transformed into real customers, it is useful for every company to organize events, conferences and live workshops.

In this way, you can constantly attract the attention of the audience and "target" your offer based on the preferences and needs of consumers.

Thanks to these 5 Lead Generation strategies you can save a lot of time to transform the leads and contacts collected into potential customers interested in your products and services. Apply them and you will be closer than ever to success.

Chapter 31

Creating your Company Blog using Wordpress

WordPress is by far the most used platform for managing corporate blogs. To proceed with the creation and management of a corporate blog, all you have to do is purchase a domain, choose a hosting service and install WordPress.

WordPress is free to download in its basic version. For a more complete service, you can purchase an SSL protocol and guarantee the security of the transfer of sensitive data. With WordPress, you have a number of templates, that is, free or paid themes to give a graphic identity to your corporate blog.

Remember that there is no optimal theme for a corporate blog that is defined in advance. Instead, you should choose a quality and functional WordPress theme, which is representative of your corporate identity.

One thing to keep in mind when creating your corporate blog is to build it making it as responsive as possible.
Almost 70% of Americans browse the contents on the web from their smartphone.

To be precise, 67% of Americans own a smartphone or tablet that they actively use to surf the web. In 2017 alone, 1.9 billion connections from smartphones and tablets were recorded, already greater than 1.6 connections made from traditional desktop instead.

What does this mean for you?

It means that more than 25% of active web users connect only from smartphones or tablets, favoring new generation portable devices over PCs to do the following things.

- inquire and read content;
- make purchases;
- communicate on social networks;
- network or online promotion for your business.

This means that if your blog is not responsive you are neglecting 1/4 of your potential user base, which is something you do not want to do.

Having a responsive blog is now taken for granted and is considered essential by the average web user. In fact, 22% of users who surf the internet from smartphones leave a website that has obvious problems with navigation or makes viewing of contents extremely slow.

How can I tell if my blog is responsive?
At this point we must therefore ask ourselves an important question. If my blog is the main tool with which we communicate with, promote and finally sell my professionalism, my services and my products, are we sure it is optimized for browsing and reading from smartphones and tablets?

In order to have a positive answer to this question, your blog must follow these standards.

- The texts are not written with a font that is too small and you have to continually "zoom in" to read the contents well by moving along the lines;

- The images are big enough;
-
- The menu is easy to navigate;

- There are no alignment issues between the various parts of the site;

- The social sharing buttons are big enough and you do not have to zoom in to be able to share content.

Then you definitely have a responsive blog.

If you want to carry out an automatic and secure check, you can use online responsiveness verification services, such as Amiresponsive. It is a great tool that tells you whether your corporate blog is suitable for mobile interaction or not. Just enter the correct URL of your blog to check if your blog is responsive or in any case to check for any layout problems.

If your blog is not responsive, we advise you not to delay any longer. Having a responsive blog will allow you to offer your users the best experience. Here are a few steps you can take in order to make your blog more responsive and easier to interact with.

- Make sure people can read your articles comfortably. This is extremely important to create an audience that keeps coming to your blog for more and more content.

- Allow visitors to navigate through tags and categories without problems. Making sure that your blog is easy to search through is such an incredible advantage for your visitors and something you should not forget.

- Access old articles with ease. Some people may come back months after they have read one of your articles. Making sure they are easily able to find it again is a great step towards responsiveness.

- Allow your visitors to share the contents of your most recent article on the various social platforms with a simple click. This simple feature increases the engagement by a lot, so do not sleep on it.

- Allow users to easily fill out contact forms to get in touch with you. An easy communication process between you and your potential clients can be the key to your success.

Having a corporate blog is the best strategy to create value for your company and customers, even if it is by no means an easy feat and there is no ready-made recipe for doing so.

Let's recap the tips to follow to create your successful business blog.

- Establish ad hoc goals so that people become attached to your brand thanks to informative content: Why do we want to start a blog? What do we expect? What do we want to communicate?

- Knowing the potential customers interested in your business is essential because it allows you to establish the type of content to publish.

- Identify content and topics that are engaging, stimulating and consistent for users and in line with your corporate mission with the specific purpose of bringing the right people towards conversion.

- Decide the frequency of publication. Consistency and frequency are essential to be successful when starting a corporate blog.

- Create an editorial plan that helps to organize the work in a meticulous way.

- Carefully take care of the graphic layout of the blog and try to make it as consistent as possible with the visual identity of the brand or company logo.

- Promote the blog to reach the public through social media, guest blogging, pay per click promotion campaigns etc.

- The blog is a "showcase" and a space where customers can constantly interact and leave comments and feedback. Make sure it is easy for them to get in touch with you.

If a customer is not satisfied, you need to be able to handle negative feedback.

You can do this by avoiding censorship and never deleting the negative comment, as it is likely that the user will express his dissatisfaction through other channels promoting an even more negative vision of your company.

Always try to respond politely and always ask the customer the reason for the dissatisfaction. Once you have found out what the problem is, be willing to solve it. Try to make your dissatisfied customers think again about your company and keep in touch with all the blog visitors as if they were real people. Why? because they are.

Chapter 32

Google Ads for Your Blog

Now that we have discussed everything you need to know to successfully start your company blog, it is time to dive deeper into a powerful advertising tool that will allow you to increase the exposure of your company website and attract more customers.

We are talking about Google Ads.

Even today, when it comes to Google AdWords, many doubts and curiosities arise. People still don't know what it is, how to use it, how much it costs and what benefits you can get. To overcome all these problems and inform you readers, we thought of creating a small guide inside this book that explains what Google AdWords is and why you should rely on this system to earn.

AdWords is Google's paid advertising service, and is a very useful tool for promoting a company's business online. If well combined with the SEO activity that instead deals with the optimization and organic positioning of the website, it allows you to reach high numbers of new customers in a short time.

It is an advertising platform through which it is possible to publish text ads, images and videos on search results pages and on sites of the Google content network. A truly functional web marketing tool that allows you to promote your business quickly and easily but at the same time extremely productive.

Adwords advertising is based on the creation of ads that can be viewed in the first results on search engine pages or on partner sites of Google (such as YouTube). The published announcement can be video, illustrated content or simply textual content.

Through Adwords it is possible to find new customers by tracking down people who are really interested in what your business offers. In fact, the service uses targeting tools that allow you to display certain ads only to a specific target of people - and therefore potential customers - who surf the web by searching on topics related to your business.

AdWords targeting

The main Adwords targeting are of three types.

1. **Keyword targeting**. These ads are displayed based on the keywords related to your business, chosen when you created the ad. To help you use keyword targeting with AdWords, Google also provides absolutely free tools such as Google Suggestion Tool or Google Trends that allow you to understand which are the most searched words on the net among those related to your business.

2. **Topic targeting.** These ads are displayed on a large number of pages belonging to the content

network identified at the time of setting up the advertising campaign.

3. **Placement targeting**. These ads are displayed on sites that are part of the so-called "Content Network", identified on the basis of what is specified by the advertiser. When setting up the campaign, you choose sites or interests related to your business, in order to display the ad on their pages. For example, those who manage an e-commerce of food products can display their ads in known and clicked cooking blogs.

Advanced options are also available in order to achieve an even greater level of personalization (audience targeting, device targeting, language and location targeting). This allows your ads to reach even more specific targets of potential customers, increasing the chances of success of the campaign.

The reason why you should use Google ads in your social media marketing strategy

AdWords is useful for any type of company, whatever

its size and sector, as it offers a wide range of tools to increase the online visibility of your business on all devices, greatly increasing the chances of growing your own. customer package.

But let's see in detail what are the strengths of AdWords.

- **It works on Google** which is the most used search engine in the world. With a single advertising platform you can reach a large number of users. It is aimed at a personalized target and allows you to publish ads for geo-localized searches.

- **It has flexible costs.** The company decides how much it wants to spend and how. There are no minimum access budget levels. Through the "pay per click" system, payment occurs only when users click on the ad.

- **It allows you to manage the advertising campaign completely independently.** The advertiser can check the progress of the campaign at any time, interrupt it or optimize it if necessary, using dedicated reporting tools such as Analytics.

- **There are no time limits.** With Adwords it is possible to reach users interested in your product or service 24 hours a day, 365 days a year.

How to improve your business with AdWords? This is such a great question. In fact, we have seen what AdWords is, how it works and what its strengths are, but how can you best use it to improve your company's business?

Since this is an extremely customizable web marketing tool, based on the different goals of each company it is possible to resort to one of the types of advertising campaigns made available by AdWords. Those are the following.

- **AdWords Search Campaign**. This type of campaign displays ads in correspondence with relevant Google searches carried out by users potentially interested in your business.

- **Display AdWords campaign.** This type of campaign allows you to increase your company's visibility on the web towards potential new customers who will view the ad on sites owned by Google (Gmail, YouTube, Blogger, etc.) or that collaborate with Google.

- **AdWords Remarketing Campaign.** This type of campaign promotes the company to users who have previously visited its site.

- **AdWords Shopping Campaign.** This type of campaign allows you to promote the company's products by offering users detailed information before they click on the ad.

An AdWords advertising campaign always proves to be a useful choice to increase your business, but to be successful it is very important to make the most of all the tools it offers in a personalized way, taking into account the needs and characteristics of your company, of the market you are operating in and the target audience.

Chapter 33

Create Your First Google Ad

You have decided to create an online ad to direct users to your site when they are looking for what you offer. Where to start?

Google Ads gives you the ability to create text, image, display, mobile and many more ads. In this guide, we'll focus on making text ads and how to schedule, set up and write them so potential customers know your business is worth considering to find, do, buy what they need. In this chapter you are going to learn how to create a new text ad.

If you've just learned how to create an ad on Google,

don't worry - we'll start with the basics.

What is Google Ads?

As we have discussed in the previous chapter as well, Google Ads is a Google advertising service for businesses that want to show ads on Google search results and their advertising network.

Let's take a look at how you can actually go ahead and create your first ad for your company blog.

1. The basics

Sign in to your Google Ads account at

1 - Select the desired campaign and click on the "Ads" tab.

2 - Click on the "New Ad" tab and select "Text Ad".

At this point, you can enter a text or message for the ad you are creating. A text ad is made up of a few elements, which you can set up at this stage.

- **Title**. This is the most prominent part of the

ad, at least in terms of text size, and is the first approach to potential customers. The title should clearly state what your business is about or what products and services it offers.

- **Descriptive lines**. The description should provide more details on the products and services offered or highlight the advantages for the user who visits your site.

- **Display URL.** The display URL is not the actual page that users will be redirected to when they click on your advertisement. This link, which generally corresponds to the home page of the site, is the one that users see in the ad: it therefore represents a sort of "signature" on the web of your business.

- **Destination URL.** This is the exact page where you are directed to those who click on your ad. It should always be as relevant as possible to the search terms associated with it.

There is a maximum number of characters that can be

used for each of these items. Remember that the character count always includes spaces. Here are the different limits for the above mentioned parts of the ad.

- Title: 25 characters
- Descriptive line 1: 35 characters
- Descriptive line 2: 35 characters
- Display URL: 35 characters. If the URL is longer, it will be displayed in an abbreviated form.

Below we will see in detail how to best use these spaces to create a clear, effective and captivating online ad for potential customers. Now that you know the basics of creating a text ad, let's take a look at some tips that can come in handy.

2. Relate to customers

It may seem simple. Yet, to create a message that responds to customer needs, first of all it is necessary to identify them clearly. When and why should people search for your products or services? What is your main target demographic? What expectations do consumers have of your business? What do your current customers say when they leave the store or what aspects do they like the most?

The answers to these questions will help you understand what writing style to adopt in your ads, but also to identify any products, services or offers that deserve to be highlighted. Try using some adjectives that you think describe your business or your way of serving customers.

3. Help your business stand out

You can take a look at online ads from businesses similar to yours to get an idea of how your industry presents itself to customers who are looking for the products or services you offer. This is a great way to understand what messages or strategies are working in your field, but also to learn how to create an online ad that stands out from the rest. Do not copy a competitor's ad. Your business is unique, as should your way of communicating with customers.

A good tactic is to use the ad to highlight your "value proposition", which is the quality of your offering and what sets your business apart from others. What extra benefits do you offer to your customers? Free shipping? Expert advice on an exclusive product or technology? A long experience in your sector? If you're writing an ad for a special promotion, include its value in your ad text. For example, you might tell potential customers that they can "save 50%" on your site, that there is a "seasonal sale" in progress, and so on.

4. Call users to action

When creating an online ad, a good strategy to consider is to include a "call to action" - a clear and concise message, centered around a dynamic verb, that tells the reader what you would like them to do after seeing your ad. Some call to actions that you can use when creating your first Google ad are the following.

- Buy now
- Place an order
- Book now
- Buy today
- Find out more
- Call now
- Sign in
- Request a quote

Notice how these call-to-action phrases are specific about the next step, what the customer should do to close a deal with your company. Added to this is a sense of urgency, thanks to words like "today" or "now".

If applicable to your business or products, you can reinforce the sense of urgency by giving customers a time limit to join your offer. In the ad description, you can write something like "Valid only in August" or "Promotion ends on a specific date". Taking advantage of the seasonality of a product can be another way to encourage people to take action now. Do you sell costume accessories? Try writing an ad focusing on this product category in the weeks leading up to Halloween or Carnival. If you sell gift items and have a lot of sales over the holiday season, start advertising your offer starting in November, when Christmas shopping already begins.

5. Focus on the details

The ad should clearly explain what the user will find on your site. In particular, the first page that the user will visit, known as the "landing page", should be relevant to both the ad text and the search terms associated with it.

To create an effective online ad, a good practice is to write different text for each ad group. Ad groups refer to specific themes, topics or products, through which you can efficiently organize your campaign. For example, if you are involved in interior design, you could create an ad group called "home design", one on "office design" and another on "event design".

Instead of writing a single common ad, which speaks generically about your interior design services, think about specific text for each ad group. This foresight will make your ads more relevant to those who are looking for a particular product or service. Returning to the example, the ad "home design" should lead the user to a page on interior design services for individuals, not to mention event or office set-ups which, for this keyword, are irrelevant. If you are advertising a specific promotion, you can include it in the ad group by writing text that aims to highlight the offer, as discussed above.

6. Short and clear is best

Remember that Google Ads text ads are relatively short. If you're thinking of using a catchphrase or pun, this probably isn't the best place to do it. The ad must serve your business to present itself in a clear and precise way, so that people know that your offer matches exactly what they are looking for.

7. Include keywords

If you've already set up your Google Ads account, you know that keywords match the terms people search for on Google when they're looking for something. It is the keywords that trigger the publication of your ad, for relevant search results. That's why using keywords you've associated with a particular ad group in text immediately increases its relevance.

Returning to the example, let's assume that one of your keywords is "home design". By including "home design" in your ad title, you grab the attention of users, highlighting how your offer matches exactly the term they just searched for. It can also be effective to end the text with variations of the keyword, such as "home design".

That said, you don't need to write separate text for every single keyword associated with your campaign. Try to find the main theme of your ad group and write some text that includes the keyword you think is the most representative.

By following these tactics, you can be sure your Google ads will be extremely effective. However, do not forget that only by testing what works and what does not for your company you will be able to find the perfect recipe for your ads. This is true for Facebook ads and Youtube ads as well.

We encourage you not to be afraid of experimenting with your ads, as each time you will get better and gather more and more experience on what works and what should be avoided. As for everything in life, reading about Google ads will only get you this far. You have to put in practice what you have learned in order to get positive results.

If you do not want to commit yourself to this learning process, you can always decide to delegate this part to an advertising agency that will take care of your ads for you. Our experience tells us that it is always better to have at least a little grasp of what is happening behind the scenes, before delegating it to external agencies. In fact, this will help you better understand what they are doing and communicate with them in a much more effective way.

Chapter 34

Bing Ads

How does Bing Ads work? For your online searches, you will most likely use the Google search engine. If, on the other hand, you are part of that percentage of users who also see beyond Big G, you will have come across Bing. This search engine is developed by Microsoft and is trying, with a lot of effort, to surpass the number one Search Engine, revolutionizing digital search.

The goal is ambitious, however, Bing differs significantly from Google when it comes to its Pay Per Click (or PPC) ads.

What is a Pay Per Click ad? Pay Per Click ads are "a form of search engine marketing (SEM) in which the advertiser pays for each click made by users on the ads".

While Google Ads offers simple and intuitive features for building PPC campaigns, Bing Ads has unique advantages that stand out from the search engine giant.

Bing's PPC ads work on Microsoft's three most popular search engines: Bing, Yahoo, and AOL. When you create a campaign on Bing your content is shared across all these platforms at the same time. With over five billion monthly searches on the Microsoft network, this makes Bing PPC a notable marketing tool for paid advertising campaigns.

In practical terms, Bing's PPC ads work in a similar way to Google's ads. Here are the similarities with Google ads.

- Bid on certain keywords based on their traffic volume;
- Your ad appears when that keyword is searched;
- You pay Bing every time a visitor clicks on your

ad;

- Like on Google, your ad text can be up to 80 characters long, plus, Bing also has support tools that can help your team build a cost-effective keyword list, so you never lose money on ads that don't come displayed.

With Bing, you can also set up targeting filters that determine where and when an ad will appear. For example, if you want your ad to appear on mobile devices only, you can select the mobile traffic option. Or, if you want your ad to run exclusively on Yahoo, you can filter it from Bing and AOL. This gives your team more flexibility and maximizes the effectiveness of your PPC campaign.

Bing's PPC Ads represent a timely opportunity for marketing teams. In fact, Bing is less competitive than Google AdWords and its users buy 36% more online than any other search engine. While Google Ads is still a very powerful tool, there are some benefits of Bing that make it attractive to small and medium-sized businesses. Now that you understand how Bing PPC ads work, let's see some of the main differences between

Bing PPC and Google AdWords.

While both Bing PPC and Google AdWords allow you to filter your ad targeting, Bing's software has a unique innovation that sets it apart from Google. With Bing, you can set age filters for your search ads so that only visitors from a certain age group can see them. On the other hand, on Google Adwords, you can set a position filter so that visitors from a certain part of the world see your content. With this targeting possibility, your marketing campaigns will be seen by a qualified and interested audience.

Another feature that sets Bing apart is its social media extension. The social media extension is a line of text in your ad that indicates to the visitor the number of social media followers of your business. This is especially useful for those with a greatsocial presence to show their authority and popularity online. On the other hand, Google AdWords could only show the number of followers of Google+, a now defunct social.

True, Google Ads does not have social extensions, but its ads can still be enriched with a lot of other information.

According to Microsoft, Bing accounts for over 34% of the global desktop search engine market. This means that roughly one in three people prefer to use Bing over other search engines, and most importantly, Bing's PPC ads potentially reach 60 million users that Google can no longer intercept.

In terms of reach, Google remains the search engine of choice for over 75% of users. This, however, doesn't mean that Bing isn't worth your investment. Bing has over 137 million users who search around six billion times a month. According to recent analysis, Bing users tend to be older than Google users and have an income of over $ 100,000 per year. So even though Google has a larger audience, Bing works with users who have a much more significant purchasing power.

Users engagement

Analyzing those who have already tested Bing PPC, it was found that Bing ads recorded a 34% higher click-through rate than Google ads. The products that work best on this search engine are financial and commercial services. This is largely attributed to the well-known financial reports from MSN and Yahoo, which produce multiple keywords related to online business and commerce relationships.

Bing users tend to be more engaged with sites even after ad clicks, and their ads run at 56% higher conversion rates than Google Adwords. This is because Bing users typically have more interest in e-commerce and are willing to spend money online.

Display and placement of the ad

Since there are fewer users on Bing, its ads tend to be higher in search results than on Google AdWords. In fact, Bing ads appear 35% higher in search results than Google ads. Bing copies Google's keyword auction technique, which favors its users because they don't have to surpass Google's massive user base. With Bing's less competitive marketplace, you won't have to bid that high on keywords to keep your place on the search results page.

Cost per Click

With fewer competitors bidding on keywords, you can expect to spend less on your Bing ads. In fact, a company spent 35% less on Bing ads than Google AdWords. In terms of Cost Per Click (CPC), ReportGarden found that, for a set of financial industry keywords, the average CPC for Bing was $ 7.99 while that of Google was $ 20.08. Because overall traffic is lower on Bing, CPC is generally less expensive. This presents an opportunity to get very positive ROI if you can capitalize on the right keyword at the right time.

Commercial value

If you're wondering what to choose between Google AdWords and Bing PPC, you need to know that both tools can be invaluable assets for your social media marketing strategy.

As we have seen in the previous chapter, with Google, you have access to a large audience targeted on specific demographics (by geographic area) and you can trust that your content will appear on the most used search engine in the world. However, this space is highly competitive and you will need to diligently monitor your campaign if you want to see a positive return on your investment. Your marketing team will need a lot of tools and experience to make Google AdWords a reliable source of lead generation.

On the other hand, Bing PPC presents a low-risk option for paid ad campaigns. You still have access to a large audience, but the keyword bidding isn't as competitive as Google. The trade-off here is that Bing's traffic is significantly lower than Google's. Therefore, while your ads may rank higher and cost less, they may not be seen by as many people. This limitation can discourage larger companies with larger marketing budgets.

Now that you understand the strengths and weaknesses of these two search engines and the potential of each for PPC campaigns, you must know that these alone are not enough. To get your online business off the ground, you need to create a complete inbound marketing strategy.

Chapter 35

Inbound marketing

What is inbound marketing? It is the new method to find customers online, exploiting the potential of the web. Traditional marketing (called outbound) is based on the invasive interruption in user activities to display an advertisement, such as telemarketing, events, fairs, advertisements in specialized magazines or newspapers. Outbound no longer works as well as it once did. In fact, it has a very low return on investment (ROI) and often ends up irritating those who have seen the ads. Inbound, on the other hand, focuses on creating educational content that is interesting to the potential customer so as to attract them to your website.

When it comes to inbound marketing, it is not your

company that goes to the potential customer, but it is the customer that comes to your company. A pretty important difference.

What is inbound marketing?

Inbound marketing is a method of finding customers online that is based on 2 pillars:

1. Content. Create online content (web pages, blog posts, videos and much more) optimized for SEO, therefore for search engines, so that a user can find us, and the use of social media to have greater visibility.

2. Context. Understanding which contents can most attract visitors and studying a personalized strategy with messages and promotions that will then be shared through the website, blog and social channels.

It is very important for a company to be present online: almost all users who surf the net perform searches in search engines. On Google alone, there are 54,000 searches per second. Just try to figure this number in your mind, it is truly amazing.

The environment is very competitive, and for this you have to do everything possible to get the results as soon as possible.

First of all, your website must be responsive. On the other hand, most of the searches are carried out by mobile and (rightly) Google rewards responsive websites, showing them in the first places of the first page.

Then, develop a blog about your business. Nourish it by posting periodically and offering useful content that your customers will want to read. The blog is a business card that will allow you to both attract visitors and gain authority, being recognized as true experts in the sector.

Research the right keywords in order to SEO optimize all your articles. But be careful, because keywords are no longer enough: we need to develop a content strategy that can be interpreted by search engines.

Now that you have your visitors, you are ready to convert them into contacts, so you can profile them and know for sure what their needs and aspirations are.

But how do you convert them? How do you find the data and information you need?

You will need to create landing pages, with a form in which they will enter their data, CTAs to entice them to take an action and a thank you page.

But that's not all. For a visitor to fill out the form, you will have to offer something in return. In fact, in the so called "thank you" page you will have to insert useful and quality content, such as guides and videos, and in the landing specify what you are going to offer and what benefit the information you give will bring. Be careful, however, not to overdo it. It must be simple and intuitive.

Now that contacts are in your database, only one, but decisive, phase is missing for them to become your customers.

Everything hinges on content. You need to create targeted content, based on what your contacts have told you by filling out the forms. You can do so by using DEM (direct email marketing) campaigns combined with efficient workflows through a crm.

If you are wondering what the last sentence means, a crm (customer relationship management) manages your contacts through a path called workflow; the workflow, based on the actions performed by the contact, performs other actions to feed our contact with content. In most cases, personalized emails are sent at predetermined intervals with videos, guides, articles or other content suitable for closing a sale.

Once the contact has been nurtured enough, he will ask you for advice or wish to purchase your product. And this can happen all automatically once you have set up the system.

Now that the customer has bought, please don't throw its contact into oblivion. A satisfied and "delighted" customer is a great promoter who will attract new potential customers or purchase more himself.

Not sure how to delight a customer? Just keep a good relationship with him. Invite him to leave reviews, or shoot an interview so that he can express his opinion of your product. In this way, he will feel very important because you will show that you are interested in his experience of your service or product, and you will have a great testimonial in return for doing so.

You can also organize events to invite him to, and continue to create smart content specifically addressed to him on your site. In fact, there are web pages that change according to who views them thanks to the marketing automation tools we explained to you earlier and with social media, monitoring conversations and interactions.

Nourishing the relationship with your customer is fundamental to be profitable long term, please do not forget it and keep doing it consistently.

Chapter 36

Outbound Marketing

In outbound marketing the advertising message is "pushed out" on the market, in order to track the attention of potential customers through advertising in the media in general and through in-person contact.

The typical channels of outbound marketing are print media, billboards, newspapers, flyers, cold calls, radio, TV, banners, emails, popups on websites.

Outbound Marketing is based on the principle that the marketing messages generated by the company are sent through various channels so that the right message reaches the right person at the right time, interrupting them in a certain sense in their daily life. For this, it is also referred to as Interruption Marketing, because it literally interrupts what people are doing to catch their attention.

Outbound Marketing was pretty much the only way to market products until recently, particularly before the revolution brought by the Internet. Think of a traditional market, where merchants couldn't just sit back and wait to be joined by customers. In an era like that, merchants first of all had to "announce" that they were in possession of certain products or services. Not only that. They did not have easily searchable user bases like today's online audiences, and they also needed to make more noise than their competitors to get people's attention. For this reason they aimed to exploit the power of the mass media, such as newspapers, radio, television, to get noticed by the widest possible audience.

It is easy to understand how outbound marketing, also defined as traditional marketing, still makes use of this same method today, as it "hunts" customers through a communication that today is defined as extended and one-way.

We must recognize outbound marketing at least 3 strengths.

The ability to reach "unexpected" customers. Especially during the running-in phases of a startup, sending emails or phone calls to an unknown recipient could bring good results, namely the acquisition of new customers.

The collection of information. Phone calls (cold calls, so called because they are made to people never seen or heard before, therefore "cold"), can be an effective method to generate sales, at least at first, as they allow you to find information on the field customers of products and services.

The offline focus. Flyers, billboards, posters do not necessarily require digital support and are still widely used. The same goes for TV and radio. True, it is no longer possible to live without the internet, but there are contexts, such as local businesses and trade fairs, in which the "offline" contact with the potential customer still has a notable effect.

However, among the limitations of this strategy there are quite a few points to keep in mind.

Costs. Printing flyers, billboards, banners, newspapers has a very high price if we compare it to digital media. Same thing if you think about broadcasting a commercial on TV or on the radio.

Difficult to track the ROI. With Outbound Marketing it is particularly difficult to calculate the return on investment of the marketing activities that are carried out, precisely because of the lack of direct traceability of user response.

The logic of interruption. Interrupting the potential customer in his daily life, either through a banner or with a call, is always seen as a nuisance both online and offline.

Chapter 37

Inbound Marketing vs Outbound Marketing

In summary, the main differences between Outbound & Inbound Marketing are the following.

The approach to the customer. While outbound marketing sends one-way and general messages to a wide audience (which often is not interested in the message), inbound marketing creates and offers content developed specifically for an interested and specific audience, structured to be intercepted and received during the purchase phases.

The costs of advertisement. Outbound marketing relies on advertising spaces that have a considerable cost, if compared to those of inbound marketing.

ROI measurement capability. Measuring outbound marketing data is almost impossible, as there are no means capable of precisely tracking the data of users watching a commercial, for example, or a billboard. Different is the case of inbound marketing, which is based on traceable data and interactions.

The creation of value. While outbound marketing is limited to conveying the advertising message, inbound marketing tends to build a relationship of trust with the user thanks to content and interactions that add value to the target audience.

So, at this point we would not be surprised if you had a question in mind. Which is better? Let's try to give an answer to this question.

Anyone who says that it is preferable to use inbound marketing over outbound marketing, or vice versa, is giving you a partial answer. To determine which method is best for your business, you need to consider your company, your audience, and your specific marketing goals.

But one thing is certain. While inbound marketing can live without outbound marketing, it cannot be said that the opposite is true. In fact, the online world offers incredible growth opportunities for brands truly interested in offering a solution before a product, which clearly favours inbound marketing.

Conclusion

Congratulations on making it to the very end of this book, it has been a great journey.

We hope you were able to find valuable information to improve the online presence of your company or personal brand. We have tried our best to give you every tool and strategy you might need to turn your social media pages into money making machines.

Now it is on you to put in practice what you have learned. Because remember that understanding a concept and making it work for you are two totally different things and as an entrepreneur or influencer you should always be willing to take the risk to try and test new strategies.

We are sure that if you commit to seriously working on

your social media marketing strategy, you will be well ahead of competition. After all, it is not a secret that most businesses have a superficial approach when it comes to their online presence. Doing things differently will certainly put you miles ahead of them and will give you an unfair advantage in the long run.

We hope you enjoyed this book and we wish you great success!